Now Johnny Can Do Arithmetic

A Handbook on the Use of
Colored Rods

Caleb Gattegno

Educational Solutions Worldwide Inc.

The colored rods (Algebricks) and other teaching material described in this book are obtainable from: www.EducationalSolutions.com

First American edition published in 1971. Reprinted in 2010.

Educational Solutions Worldwide Inc.
2nd Floor 99 University Place, New York, N.Y. 10003-4555
www.EducationalSolutions.com

Table of Contents

Preface

This book was written in 1957-58, appeared in 1960 in England and soon after in French, Spanish, Portuguese, and Hebrew editions. It now exists also in German and Italian. But it was never widely read in this country although it was very popular everywhere else, as the successive printings and editions prove.

It had been kept out of reach of the public by a publishing contract which is now voided and I am able to offer an American edition to parents and teachers as in other parts of the world.

However much I changed over the years this book has kept for me a freshness and an adequacy which prevented me from having to recast it as was the case for a number of my earlier works, some of which I had to withdraw from the market because I had no time to re-write them.*

---

* For example: From Actions to Operations, A Teacher's Introduction, Teaching Mathematics in an Expanding Economy, no longer available.

'Now Johnny' was originally intended to help parents in the home, but teachers decided to adopt it and now it is one of the texts of mine they like best. The few hundred American teachers who read it in its English version were among those to encourage me to go ahead with this edition.

A companion volume containing colored diagrams is available at the same time under the title of *Arithmestics* and could illustrate a number of statements of this book.

No doubt readers will be helped if while studying this text they manipulate the rods from a box of Algebricks.

Caleb Gattegno
New York City, 1970

1 An Astonishing Invention

This book is written for the people who want to know why children have difficulty with arithmetic, and who would like to do something about it.

Over twenty-five years ago, in Belgium, a schoolmaster wondered why small children could pick up and remember tunes so easily whereas they found it so difficult to understand arithmetic and to remember what they were taught. Mathematicians are often musicians, but this is not what Georges Cuisenaire had in mind. He himself played the violin and taught music as well as arithmetic; but he was no mathematician. His question was not about mathematics — it was about *learning*, and he set out to find an aid to the learning of arithmetic that 'resembled' a musical instrument. At last he found what he was looking for.

This book tells in simple language how you can gain the full advantage of his astonishing invention for the child in whom you are interested.

Cuisenaire was born in Thuin, a Belgian town of historical interest and great charm. He spent all his life there, teaching in and directing schools. He won several decorations for his services in the two world wars, but posterity will remember him not for this, but because he enabled us to break free from the deeply-rooted prejudice that it is normal for most children to dislike arithmetic and to be poor at it.

In 1953 I joined Cuisenaire in the task of spreading the knowledge of his discovery. Cuisenaire had gone straight to the heart of this centuries-old problem and found the simple but revolutionary tool that made it possible for every child to do well in arithmetic. My part was to enquire why it was so successful and, having found the answer, to develop and refine. I wish, once more, to acknowledge my deep gratitude to the genius of Cuisenaire.

My contribution has been to recognize and link together the value of his invention and an awareness of how it could become related to the whole teaching of mathematics. The relationship depends on an acceptance of the principle The Subordination of Teaching to Learning.

You may ask yourself what it is that stops Johnny being good at arithmetic when Peter manages so well. Surely this must point to a difference in their inborn aptitude. Does Johnny lack the mathematical bent that Peter was lucky enough to possess from birth? That is what the teachers say, and it seems to make good sense.

Of course, even with colored rods and an advanced approach to learning, Peter may be quicker than Johnny, but Johnny can be infinitely better than he was — and so can Peter. In any case, why should we compare Johnny with Peter when we know that their lives will be quite different? What we must do is to clear away the obstacles we adults have placed in Johnny's path so that he can meet arithmetic with a free and confident mind and enjoy it just as Peter does, even if he will never attain the heights of which Peter is capable.

We shall not discuss aptitudes, however, because we should only lose sight of our main theme, which is that Johnny *can* do well at arithmetic and that you can prove this for yourself in a few hours.

What did you and I (and Johnny) go through when we began to learn arithmetic? Ask anyone what must be done first in arithmetic and they will tell you it is learning to count. We begin with the unit and, by learning to count, we are supposed to acquire 'number sense.'

So Johnny learns to count, perhaps up to ten, and then he is ready to learn to add. Because he began by counting, he will automatically add by counting: 3 and 2 make 5 because you can count up from 3 by two steps to get the answer: '3 (4) 5.' It is not so simple to add 3 and 5, but Johnny works his way up — '3 (4, 5, 6, 7) 8,' and once again he gets the right answer. But it is easy to lose count on the way, so he uses his fingers. We did the same at his age, which shows that our arithmetic, too, was based on counting.

The teacher finds it 'shameful' that Johnny should use his fingers. He ought to know at once that 3 and 5 are 8, without going through this process of counting up from 3 by five steps to reach the answer.

This is the first obstacle to progress, and it is we who have placed it on the child's path. We spend a long time establishing counting as the basis for addition and, when we have succeeded, we forbid children to use it and insist upon answers being given without counting. It is no wonder that some children never recover from such treatment and that others develop a resentment against a subject in which, as soon as a skill has been acquired, it becomes shameful to use it.

If this were the only obstacle far fewer children would fall by the wayside. But now the teacher begins to teach multiplication and, for weeks, Johnny learns, recites, and tries to apply the so-called multiplication tables. Once again, he is required to rely upon a rhythmic activity to fix in his memory what he is supposed to learn. Instead of one, two, three . . . he now chants: 'two ones are two, two twos are four, two threes are six . . .'

At last he knows them, and the teacher asks him to find the cost of six apples at 5 cents each. Johnny says to himself, 'six ones are six, six twos are twelve, six threes are eighteen . . .' and so on until he reaches 'six fives are thirty.' But this is the same 'shameful' pattern he used when adding by counting, and the teacher insists that he ought to know the answer at once.

Why, then, did he learn the tables? The teacher's answer is, how else could one know that six fives are thirty? This is not how Johnny sees it, for he is being consistent when he uses what he has been taught to help him to solve the problems he is given. Yet when he does so, it displeases the teacher! So he gives up the struggle and assumes that he must be stupid because he can do only what he understands and not something quite different that is required of him.

We should remember that young children have plenty of scope for spontaneous activity in play and, here, suffer little interference from adults. In their play they know they can freely use what they learn, and they enjoy exercising the skills acquired. This does not seem to apply to work at school, and they find themselves living in two worlds — the world of play and the world of schoolwork — in which the rules are different. In the play-world the rules make sense; in the school-world these rules break down and become obstacles placed in their way just when they feel ready to go forward to use what they know.

If we do not want children to add by counting we should not begin by teaching them to do so and, if we do not want them to go through their tables to find the product they need for a multiplication, we must refrain from teaching multiplication by way of memorizing tables.

These are two examples amongst many we could find which show what problems we create for our children, and parents will be able to recall what they themselves experienced through them.

There is another example which results from the way in which Johnny is expected to do subtraction.

Subtraction is looked at as addition in reverse, and is seen to be possible whenever the number to be subtracted is smaller than the other number. When we come across a subtraction such as 321−274, it is clear that this condition applies but, when Johnny sets out to find the answer, he faces an awkward problem. He must begin his subtraction with the units and he cannot subtract 4 from 1.

To meet this problem he is taught one of the three methods that have been devised to make this perfectly possible subtraction feasible. For centuries, teachers have debated the merits of the three methods, and have introduced variations in each, in the hope of making their chosen method acceptable to the mind of the child. If, after a painful struggle, they succeed, a change of school — or even of class — may mean that the child finds his fellows using a different method he cannot understand and, if he is required to conform, he becomes confused.

We shall see, later on, that there is no need to use any of these artificial methods and that Johnny can, without hesitation, tackle any subtraction and understand what he is doing. For him 321−274 will seem no more difficult than 374−221.

Fractions and mixed numbers are the next pitfall for Johnny. There is no reason why this should be so, for, with the colored rods, he will meet fractions from the beginning — even before he can count — and he will know what his teacher is talking about when the time comes and will, himself, be able to talk about fractions with confidence and ease.

In short, Johnny's inability to enjoy mathematics and to become efficient in all its branches does not lie in him but in certain assumptions which we have accepted long since and which remained unchallenged until Cuisenaire began to wonder why his pupils found it so much more difficult to master the patterns made by numbers than the patterns made by sounds.

Now that we have learned what our mistakes are, and know that Johnny can tackle numbers in a way that makes sense to him, there is no reason why the mysteries of mathematics should remain obscurities for him, and no reason for him to imagine that Peter has some special powers that he himself was denied.

The first step we must take is to obtain a set of colored rods. Let your boy (or girl) play freely with them and watch what he does. You will learn much you never knew about him — his inventiveness, his endless capacity to renew his games, his sense of pattern, and the way in which, *while playing*, he picks up the essential concepts upon which mathematics is based. You will discover that he has an astonishing memory for abstract facts and a natural skill in mastering the relationships he finds exemplified in the colors and sizes of the rods. Because his mind is young and fresh he may well be quicker at this than you are yourself, and this will give him great encouragement.

If, as you watch, you gain a new respect for your child's intellectual powers and creative ability, this book will have fulfilled an important part of its purpose. But it will do much more. It will free you of your own anxieties about numbers and about Johnny's ability to handle them. The discoveries you make with him will challenge your mind as well as his and, like him, you will find a new enthusiasm.

One word more. Parents are rightly anxious not to risk confusing their children at school by teaching them methods that differ from those used there. No such danger exists with the rods. They are a means of understanding how numbers behave and this is something to which *every* method has to conform. What Johnny does with the rods at home will make sense of what he is taught about numbers at school.

Nor is there the least fear that your child will become dependent upon the rods. The very opposite is the case, for they enable him to gain an independence and a mental curiosity that are the marks of the truly mathematical mind — and this is powerfully fostered from the very beginning.

2 Getting to Know the Material

When you buy your set of Algebricks and the materials that can be used with them, you should not try at once to relate them to arithmetic. The important thing is to become familiar with them, and this is achieved through games.

1 Free Play

Because these games need to be free, they will only achieve their maximum value if no one directs them.

Empty a set on the table or floor and let the rods suggest what to do. Children are so quickly absorbed by their own constructions, and can produce so many objects and patterns — whether flat or in three dimensions — that no list can suggest what is possible.

I have seen children (and, in this, parents are children, too) make creative combinations which so pleased them that I could not induce them to break up what they had done to make something else. These constructions can be so fascinating, not only to the child but to his parents, that it may be worth taking a color photograph of the 'work of art' to keep as a memory of the child's achievement, and this will heighten his sense of the value of what he has produced.

What do children produce *in general?*

No one can foretell what a child will do, and what I shall describe does not represent what children *should* do. Who can claim, even after seeing thousands of children playing with the rods, that the hundreds of millions of children he has never seen will do this or that when confronted with a set of colored rods?

What I have seen is that children begin either by making flat patterns or by putting a few rods upright to form a porch or an arch, a cross or a wall. The horizontal patterns may be solid or may consist of outlines. If solid, they are either done for the fun of the color-patterns that result, or to make familiar objects such as a staircase or the wall of a house with doors and windows. These flat constructions are the equivalent of the paintings that children like to do on paper.

If the child chooses to do an outline, it may be a railway line, a fence enclosing a ranch complete with house and cattle, or it may be the name of the child, or a train that is straight or one that winds about.

The choice of colors is an important factor in the construction and often gives an indication of the mood of the child at the time. In a village where there had been an accident, all the children next morning used dark colors and severe outlines, many being churches and crosses. The sadness in the atmosphere was reflected in both the colors and patterns chosen.

A child whose mother had been taken away that morning, and who refused to cry, revealed what he felt in the construction he made with his rods. Another, aged six, who belonged to a military family and evidently had heard much about weapons, produced a cannon which was in all respects a wonderful piece of art. The rods balancing upon each other, with colors, dimensions and proportion so perfectly apt, showed a profound, even if intuitive, knowledge.

To help a child to develop through such spontaneous games, we must leave him alone to work out what he is doing, looking at what he produces with respect and understanding. If he goes on repeating the same pattern we must watch him closely and try to discern whether he is attempting to overcome some technical difficulty or whether he is working out some recurrent image that is troubling his emotional life. We can help him to change the direction of his interest by playing with him and introducing some new idea which he may wish to adopt, or which may suggest something quite new to him.

Watching children at play is the best possible source of information we have as to the personality that emerges when engaged in creative activity and in the investigation of the environment. Parents can help most by not interfering but by offering new possibilities for the child's imagination to work on.

In the course of this free play, the child learns many things about the rods upon which, later on, he will be building his mathematical knowledge. He will discover

1   that rods of the same color are equal in length;

2   that those of the same length have the same color;

3   that those with different colors have different lengths;

4   that if he wishes to make equal lengths he can only do so by putting particular rods end to end;

5   that the rods have been so made that whatever he constructs corresponds to a number of white rods.

It is important not to point out these things to the child and not to expect him to *say* that he knows all this. The parent will know what the child has discovered by observing that he is making use of this knowledge.

2 Games of Recognition by Size

1   This game can be played by one or more children or the whole family, and it introduces them to the directed play which increases still further their familiarity with the material.

Each player holds a white rod and a red rod in his hand behind his back. Each is asked to produce either the white rod or the red one.

This is so easy that after the age of three it ceases to be a game unless we add a light green rod as well. The children will not always be right the first time. After a while the pink rod is added, and when the hand can hold it, a yellow rod is added too.

This game is extremely popular and it enables a child, first by comparison and then in the absolute, to know which rod is which by 'feel' alone. Except with the color-blind child, selection by sight is easy, and to be asked to pick up this rod or that is no challenge; but to know the color of a rod by touch is evidence of an important mastery of the material. Incidentally, color-blind children are not at such a disadvantage in using the rods as might be supposed. Even if they cannot recognize the colors, they can often distinguish them by shades and can always do so by length. They accept the color-names as readily as children with normal sight and appear to enjoy the compensation of a greater sensitivity to this factor of length. Indeed teachers and parents may not become aware of the color-blindness at all.

When this mastery is achieved with five rods, we can repeat the game, adding a dark green, and then a black, followed by a tan. The actual number of rods a child can hold will depend upon the age of the child, and at a certain point we shall have to discard one rod when we add another.

So long as the game continues to present a challenge, and a challenge to which the child can respond successfully, the interest of the game is sustained. New rods must not be added too quickly, but it is equally important to observe when a new rod must be introduced to maintain the challenge.

2 The next game is to place a single rod in the child's hand behind his back. He is asked to feel it well before saying anything and, when he has made up his mind, to say what its color is. He then looks at it to see whether he was right.

If he is consistently wrong it shows that he is not yet ready for this game and must go back to the earlier game. It will help him if we let him compare what he sees when the rod is before his eyes with what he feels when it is behind his back. Another variation, which helps when a child finds this difficult, is to place just two rods in his hand so that he can make use of the comparison that each affords in deciding what the other is called.

The purpose of this game is to consolidate the absolute knowledge of the rods which he began to acquire in the first game.

3 One of each of the rods is placed on a tray (the lid of the box will serve well) and this is held by the child on his head. He is then asked to produce a rod of some specified color. This can be played at first with a smaller number of rods to make it easier.

A variation, which a number of children can play when they have become proficient at this, is to place a number of rods in a bag and ask the children in turn to bring out the rod which they first touch, announcing its color before it is displayed. Or they can be asked to feel around until they find a named rod. The latter variation permits of comparison but the former calls for the absolute knowledge of each rod.

4   If the child has mastered the challenges presented by these three games, he is ready to tackle a new one which involves the substitution of two rods for one, or one rod for two.

We give him one rod and ask him to give us the name of two rods that together make its length. Or we give him two rods and ask for the name of the single rod that is equal to these when put end to end.

This game will be enjoyed only when mathematical judgment is beginning to appear and success will be achieved only after practice at the earlier games. But success shows that the child is now well on the way to arithmetical insights.

3 Imagery Games

If we arrange the rods in order of length, side by side, we form a 'staircase,' and games based upon this experience of producing order in terms of length are of the greatest value.

1   The child is first asked to name the rods of the staircase from the smallest to the largest by their colors: white, red, light green, pink, yellow, dark green, black, tan, blue and orange. He then shuts his eyes and tries to say what he still remembers. He is successful when he can go up the staircase and down again correctly.

2   Having succeeded in this, he is asked to name the rods in order, but missing one each time: white, light green, yellow, black, blue and, returning, orange, tan, dark green, pink, red.

3   A rod is named (by color) and the child is asked to name the next in order, first upwards and then downwards. This game, like the others, is played with eyes shut.

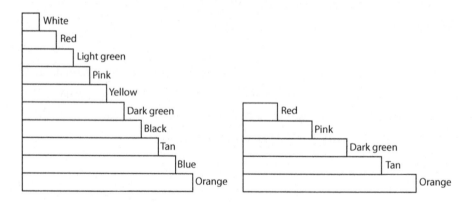

4 Number Games

The child, having gained familiarity with the rods, is now ready to identify them by number-names, and these are introduced by a code. Up till now, he has identified the rods by color and length, and now he will recognize them by *place.* Looking at the staircase, he can see that the white rod is the *first* step of the stairs, the red rod the *second,* the light green the *third,* and so on up to the orange which is the *tenth.*

We shall begin by calling the white rod *one,* the red *two,* and so on up to the orange, which is *ten.*

This is still not arithmetic: it is language. But the staircase makes sense of the language. The child is not just 'learning to count'; he is learning number-names just as he learned the color-names of the rods but he can see why these names fall into the order they do when they are used in counting.

It is not necessary for the child to realize this. All he needs to do is to enjoy playing the games of attaching the correct number-name to each rod in turn. The rods must not be marked, for this would destroy the value of the games and is quite unnecessary. Each rod already carries its own 'marking' by being the size it is and by having its own particular relationship to all the other rods.

Here then, are a few number games, and many more can be made up:

1   Using the staircase, the rods are named by the parent (or an older child who knows the numbers) and Johnny is then asked to name them himself. Rods are produced, one by one, for him to name. This is at first done in order, up and down the staircase. As he gains confidence, they are produced at random.

2   The same game is played, but without the staircase to help, until the child can name each rod he sees.

3   As soon as it is appropriate, a written code is made: 1 for white, 2 for red, 3 for light green . . . 10 for orange.

The 'code number' is then written on a piece of paper and the child produces the corresponding rod. Where several children are playing together, one of them can write the number and the rest find the right rod.

4   More experience can be gained by using the terms *first, second, third,* etc.; The child is asked to find the seventh rod going upwards and points to the black rod in the staircase. When asked to find the seventh rod going downwards, he points to the pink. This will free the child from the belief that numerical order is only upwards.

5 The staircase can be altered by removing every second rod and re-forming those removed into a second staircase. We can then ask the same questions and use the staircases to find the answers, or, later, with eyes shut. Eventually it will be possible to play this game without using any rods at all.

Through these games the child becomes familiar with the *ordinal* numbers and, because these names are also used in fractions, we must be careful to play them both upwards and downwards, and with staircases that do not link these names forever with rods of a particular color or length.

It is important for the child to see that although 7 is linked to the black rod (because 7 white rods end to end make up its length and the white is given the value of 1), it is the seventh in the ascending series but the fourth in the descending one.

5 Trains

Games with trains introduce many important ideas and they are used extensively later on. Here it is necessary only to suggest that the child should make trains of one color so that he sees that the longer the rods are, the fewer he needs to make up a length. If one-color trains of equal length are placed side by side, many properties of the rods (which reflect the properties he will before long be noticing in numbers) will become familiar to him. One game that will keep him absorbed is to discover the smallest length for which two trains equal in length but different in color are possible and to tell how many rods are needed for each.

There is no end to the games that can be devised by both child and parent at this pre-number stage. There is no need to attempt to make up games which the parent considers will have arithmetical value. What matters is that the child should explore the possibilities of the rods and enjoy his exploration. He will discover what can be done and, equally important, what cannot be done.

The making of patterns, for example, will equip the child with experience which neither he nor the parent may ever realize was useful. These lessons of personal experience pour in through sight and touch, with color and length weaving an enduring pattern of imaginative insight. The astonishing progress in actual arithmetic which comes in the following stages is largely to be explained by this gathered wealth of ideas which, though seemingly no more than child's play, are highly charged with mathematical meaning and value.

No wonder that arithmetic itself becomes child's play and remains so — in this more serious sense — when the boy or girl faces the challenging problems of more advanced work.

3 Doing 'Real' Arithmetic

Johnny is now not only familiar with the rods but he knows them by one of their many possible number names (i.e., when all are measured by the white), and he already has a surprising store of knowledge about how numbers behave, simply through having discovered how the rods behave.

We can now play games that gather up what he has learned into a pattern he can talk about in correct mathematical language and which will enable him to see the four basic processes of arithmetic — addition, subtraction, division and multiplication — as different ways of looking at that one pattern.

Though we have to discuss these four operations separately, and one after the other, Johnny will be gaining an understanding of all of them *at the same time.* Again, although we shall be doing what is normally thought of *as work,* it will remain, for Johnny, an all-absorbing play-activity. Here are some obvious games, and Johnny and his friends will find more of their own.

Making Number Patterns

1 Addition

Take any rod and make up as many different arrangements of rods, end to end, as will make up its length exactly.

If we start with the black rod we shall find we have made a pattern of the following type:

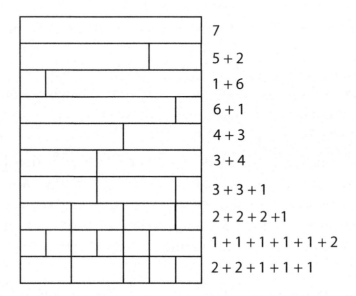

	7
	5 + 2
	1 + 6
	6 + 1
	4 + 3
	3 + 4
	3 + 3 + 1
	2 + 2 + 2 + 1
	1 + 1 + 1 + 1 + 1 + 2
	2 + 2 + 1 + 1 + 1

Of course, no two people may make the same pattern — many more lines could be added to this one, and it is fun finding them.

If, instead of the black, we choose any other rod and make its pattern, we find it has different characteristics but we can 'translate' it into numerals in the same way. If we begin with the red rod and then take, in order, light green, pink and so on upwards, we find that the possibilities are very limited at first but increase as we go forward. We need not stop at the pattern of the orange, for we can use the orange and white, the orange and red etc. The pattern of the orange and black (which is 17 when the white is 1) will contain such additions as 10 + 7, 7 + 10, 9 + 8 and 8 + 9.

Having made a pattern, one child can 'read' it and the others can, with eyes shut, check whether what he says is possible. Again, one child can call out lines he thinks will fit the chosen rod and his companion can test them by including them in the growing pattern.

This game can be played by using color-names, number-names, or the written numerals, and many variations on the theme will be suggested.

The playing of such games introduces *addition*, and it also involves the important concept of the *equation*. The symbol = can be used and translated as is *equivalent* to. Patterns can now be set out in numerals in compact form:

$$17 = 7 + 10 = 10 + 7 = 8 + 9 = 9 + 8 = 1 + 16 = 5 + 12 = 5 + 5 + 5 + 2 \ldots$$
and can be converted back into patterns of rods.

2 Addition with a Gap

While playing these addition games Johnny has quite unconsciously been learning subtractions as well, and we can now vary the games to show him that he can do this as easily as addition.

We go back to the pattern of the black rod and remove one rod from the end of each line so that the right edge is now irregular instead of straight. The rods removed are mixed and placed on one side. We are now ready for the new games:

1 The child looks at his broken pattern and finds the rod needed for each line to restore it to its original shape as a rectangle.

2 When this is done without mistakes, he is asked on a new pattern simply to say what rod is needed for each line without having the spare rods before him. If this proves too easy, he can tell us what rod is needed if we give him only the name or names of those in the unequal lines. Thus, if we say 'yellow' or 'five,' he will answer 'red' or 'two.' If we say 'white and red' or 'one and two,' he will answer 'pink' or 'four.'

When the chosen line is changed, say to blue, a new challenge is met and when success is achieved with lengths representing 15, 17 and 19, we know that Johnny is becoming an adept.

3 Before reaching these numbers we can begin to play the same games with written signs instead of rods. Here are some examples:

$$3 + ? = 7 \qquad ? + 2 = 7 \qquad 7 = 4 + ?$$

$$2 + 1 + 2 + ? = 7 \qquad\qquad 1 + 2 + ? + 3 = 7$$

If we wish to write x for the number to be found it will be no more difficult, and will pave the way for working in algebraic terms.[*]

3 Subtraction

What we have been doing can also be expressed by a new notation that goes with a new awareness:

$$7 - 3 = 4 \qquad\qquad 7 - 2 = 5$$

So we can ask our questions in this new form:

$$7 - 1 = ? \qquad 7 - ? = 2 \qquad 7 - 2 = ? \qquad 7 - ? = 3$$

The introduction of − (*minus*) in this way will be readily accepted by Johnny if we show him a pair of rods, say black and yellow, with the yellow on top of the black like this:

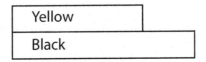

and ask him which rod he would need to cover the black section left uncovered. He knows that it is the red rod and can see that $5 + 2 = 7$ can be read as $5 + ? = 7$, or, when he sees the black

---

[*] Try here to complete the first of the Workbooks.

covered by the yellow, as 7 − 5 = ? This can also be read: what is left of the black rod when the yellow cuts off its length from it? What is left is shown as a subtraction and the answer is: it is equivalent to the red one or 7 − 5 = 2.

Each pattern provides as many subtractions as additions and the child quickly becomes used to both these ways of putting down in writing what he understands so clearly with the rods. Because he comes to know all this in play, no exercises are needed. He obtains all the practice he needs without any resort to the drill method of teaching.

By removing rods from the right or left, all the facts of addition and subtraction can be practiced, mastered and known without ever mentioning that this *is* learning.

To check progress after some time, a test can be prepared. When the answers have been written down, the child is asked to take his rods to see whether he has made any mistakes. If he has, he will correct himself. We should not expect any mistakes other than those due to haste.

Here is a test that can be used when the ten rods have been explored in the ways described in sections 1, 2 and 3:

3 + ? = 9	9 − 2 = ?	7 + ? = 9	8 + ? = 10
10 − 3 = ?	2 + ? = 10	8 = ? + 3	8 − 7 = ?

$3 + 2 + ? = 10$ $5 + ? = 9$ $9 - 1 = ?$ $2 + 4 + ? = 7$

$6 - (2 + 3) = ?$ $10 - (4 + 1) = ?$ $9 - (6 + 2) = ?$ $? - (4 + 2) = 1$

The introduction of brackets is no obstacle. They simply show that we must deal with what is inside them before going on to finish the job.

This test can be given orally as well as in writing.

Tests are themselves games and should be so presented — not as a hurdle at which Johnny may fail. If he does not succeed every time, is this not just what happens in any game? He need only try again, if need be with smaller numbers, and he can always find the elusive answer by using the rods.

Success with the ten rods can be carried forward to numbers represented by the orange and one other rod.

Here is an example of a test:

$13 - 7 = ?$ $19 - 13 = ?$ $17 - 2 = ?$ $20 - (9 + 3) = ?$

$17 + ? = 20$ $20 = 1 + ? + 10$ $14 = 7 + ?$ $15 - 8 = ?$

$6 = ? - 9$ $16 - 14 = ?$ $11 - (4 + 3) = ?$

$(4 + 5 + 7) - (3 + 2 + 8) = ?$

These are only examples, and the reader can see how easily they are made up from a pattern of rods. He can readily provide the examples that suit the child at each stage. (Cf. Workbooks.)

4 Short Division

The game we shall now play requires us to make a pattern of any chosen length by using rods of one color. Sometimes this can be done but sometimes we find we need a rod of another color to complete the length. Here is a length in which that happens in every line:

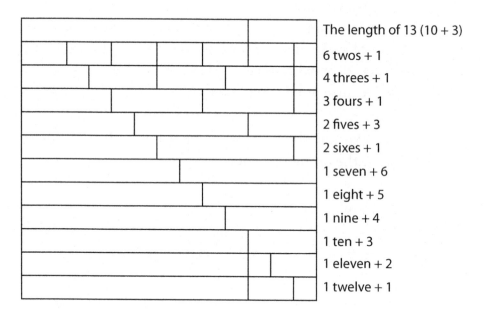

	The length of 13 (10 + 3)
	6 twos + 1
	4 threes + 1
	3 fours + 1
	2 fives + 3
	2 sixes + 1
	1 seven + 6
	1 eight + 5
	1 nine + 4
	1 ten + 3
	1 eleven + 2
	1 twelve + 1

All that is needed is to read each line after counting the rods of one color and then to see which rod completes the length.

When this is successfully done, we can ask, how many threes are there in 13? The answer will be 'four, but a white one must be added.' Or the answer may be 'four of three with one left over.'

The rod that must be added, or which we say is 'left over,' is called the *remainder*, and we read each line again in a new way. How many sixes in 13? Two, remainder 1.

We can also write what we see using the sign ×, and we can then reproduce the pattern in numerals in one long line:

$$13 = 6 \times 2 + 1 = 4 \times 3 + 1 = 3 \times 4 + 1 = 2 \times 5 + 3 \ldots$$

What we have written can be read as, 'six times two plus one equals four times three plus one' and so on.

It is essential that Johnny should be able to read and write what he sees in the pattern in all these ways and that he understands each of them equally well. It will then be easy to move forward to yet other ways of describing and writing what is seen.

Using the same pattern, we can ask how many fives in thirteen? What we already know can then be put into words as, 'thirteen divided by five equals two, remainder three,' and can be written as $13 \div 5 = 2$, remainder 3.

Once more we must make sure that this way of expressing what is known is fully understood and confidently used, and we then can introduce the further notation:

$$5\overline{)13} \quad \text{as the question,}$$

and $\quad 5\overline{)\overset{2}{13}} \quad$ as the question, with the answer shown.
$$\phantom{5\overline{)1}}3$$

It is clear that we can practice this with all the other lines of the pattern up to:

$$12\overline{)\overset{1}{13}}$$
$$\phantom{12\overline{)1}}1$$

and we can then use in the same way as many different patterns as may be needed to ensure complete confidence.

What is of utmost importance is that the various forms of notation are introduced *only when operational mastery is ensured*. The child must know what he is doing before he is expected to set down what he has done in notation. Children who approach written arithmetic in this way do not mind which notation is used and are quite ready to adopt another, such as $\frac{13}{5}$ = 2 r.3. For then it is just a matter of language, and they are already used to hearing things expressed in different ways; for example, 'It's time you were in bed,' or 'Now you must run along to bed,' or 'Off you go! You ought to be asleep.' It is the sense of what is said that matters, and variations in the words that give that sense are accepted without question.

It is also important to notice that divisions have been approached by way of addition with no need to learn multiplication tables. Moreover, it will quickly be realized that Johnny finds 13 ÷ 12 as easy as 13 ÷ 5, and the fact that 11, 12 and 13 have two figures instead of one is accepted as quite natural, without any need to mention the fact.

5 Multiplication

While doing divisions we tried to complete a length using rods of one color, and we found that with 13 it could not be done. With other lengths it can. For example, we can make up the length of the blue rod by using light green rods. We find that exactly three are required, and we can express this as follows:

$$9 = 3 \times 3, \text{ or } 3 \times 3 = 9$$

This can be expressed in other ways such as 3 times 3 is 9, or three threes are nine.

The orange rod is another example, yielding 2 × 5 and 5 × 2. Using the color names, we can say that two yellows make one orange and that five reds also make one orange. Once again, we can reverse the terms if we wish, writing in figures 2 × 5 = 10 or 10 = 2 × 5 and 5 × 2 = 10 or 10 = 5 × 2. Looking at the rods we can see why this is so.

When we look for the rods that can be matched in length by smaller rods of the same color, we find that 4, 6, 8, 9 and 10 can, whereas 2, 3, 5 and 7 cannot. Those that can, we call *composite*, and those that cannot, we call *prime*.

This is how the composite numbers can be formed:

4 with two red rods, i.e., 4 = 2 × 2

6 with three red rods or two light greens, i.e., 6 = 3 × 2 = 2 ×3

8 with four red rods or two pink, i.e., 8 = 4 × 2 = 2 × 4

10 with five red rods or two yellow, i.e., 10 = 5 × 2 = 2 × 5

There is nothing to stop us from finding whether the numbers from 11 to 20 are prime or composite. Using the rods, we discover that 11, 13, 17 and 19 are prime, and that the rest are composite and are made up as follows:

12 = 6 × 2 or 4 × 3 or 3 × 4 or 2 × 6

14 = 7 × 2 or 2 × 7

15 = 3 × 5 or 5 × 3

16 = 8 × 2 or 4 × 4 or 2 × 8

18 = 9 × 2 or 2 × 9 or 6 × 3 or 3 × 6

20 = 10 × 2 or 5 × 4 or 4 × 5 or 2 × 10

The lengths we use to form a composite length can be called the *factors* of that length, for that is the name given to the numbers those lengths represent. So, the factors of 12 are 6, 2, 4 and 3 because a length representing 12 (i.e., orange and red) can be made up of dark green, red, pink or light-green rods.

The factors of all the composite numbers from 4 to 20 can be found and written down by using the rods or by looking for them in the fines of figures we have printed above.

Let us now look at one particular composite number, say 12. We know that we can make up its length by four lines, each of one color: red, light green, pink and dark green. If we take the six red rods and place them side by side, instead of end to end, we form a rectangle. If we then take the two dark green rods and place them side by side we find we have another rectangle which has the same dimensions as the red rectangle. We can test this by placing one rectangle on top of the other to cover it exactly.

To remind us of what we have discovered, so that we do not have to keep making trains and then rectangles, we can take one of each of the rods and use them to form a cross. If we place the red across the dark green it reminds us of the dark green rectangle with its two dark green rods side by side. If we place the dark green across the red it reminds us of the six red rods side by side. Here they are, with dotted lines that show the shape of the rectangle from which the two crosses are derived:

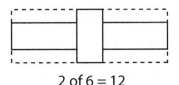
2 of 6 = 12

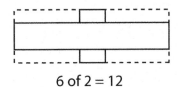
6 of 2 = 12

In just the same way, we find that the pink and light green rods form two rectangles that coincide when placed one on top of the other, and we can form two more crosses, like this:

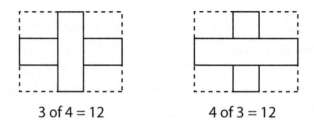

3 of 4 = 12   4 of 3 = 12

Having paired off the four factors in this way, we can show them in a single pattern, like this:

The colors opposite each other are paired together and each pair yields the number 12. Red stands for 2 and dark green for 6, and 2 × 6 = 12. Also, 6 × 2 = 12. Again, light green stands for 3 and pink for 4, and 3 × 4 = 12. Also 4 × 3 = 12.

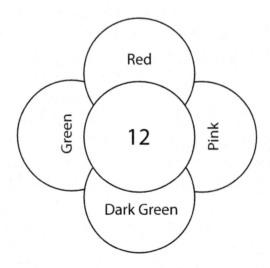

Using the pairs of colors, we can always find the number represented by using the rods to form the crosses, then the rectangles, and finally the trains, the length of which gives us the number wanted.

Here are three symbols showing patterns of this sort in a convenient form which we can use to find the three numbers represented. Two of them have only one pair of colors but the middle one has two pairs.

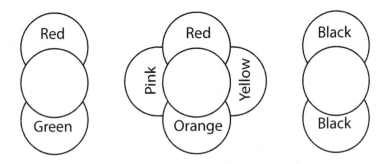

Cuisenaire chose signs like these to represent all the factors less than 10 of the composite numbers up to 100. He also devised a wall chart containing them in an arrangement that makes it easy to see how they are linked together, and, in addition, he made a pack of cards with the symbols shown separately, with counters showing the appropriate number printed on them so that the central circle of each symbol can be given the number that belongs to it. With these cardboard materials many games can be played, and children who play them do not need to 'learn their tables' because they rapidly come to know their products and factors individually.

Multiplication games can, of course, be played with the crosses as well as with the wall chart, but the Product Cards are great fun to play.

Here are some of the games that can be tried with the rods and with the cardboard materials.

1 Make a cross with any two rods and write down the *product* — which means that you write 7×8, for instance, if your cross is made with a black and a tan.

Now make the rectangle. In the example chosen, this would give seven tan rods side by side. Then set these seven rods end to end as a train and measure the length with orange rods. In this particular case there would be five orange rods and a dark green one to complete the length. We see that the length represents 56 (5 of 10 + 6) and so to complete the product we write down: $7 \times 8 = 56$.

If the cross had been tan over black, we should have had eight black rods in the rectangle and the train would have been the same length, 56, and we would write $8 \times 7 = 56$.

Make as many crosses as you wish and find the value of the product of the factors represented by the colors of the rods. Follow the same procedure:

- write down the product;
- fill in the rectangle;

- put the rods end to end;
- measure the length using the orange rods (unless the length is less than 10);
- complete your work by adding the answer you have obtained from the rods.

2 If you have the pack of cards, the counters provided will give you all the numbers equal to the products you can represent with pairs of single rods. There are 37 of them and, as we already know, some of them have two pairs of factors that can be represented by two crosses each made of two rods. In case you have not yet obtained the cardboard materials, the numbers are set out in the footnote and you can write them out on pieces of cardboard or paper.*

Now draw out a number at random and form its length with orange rods and, if necessary, one rod of a different color. Thus, if you picked out 72, you would make a length of seven orange rods and one red.

Omitting the white rod, see how many one-color trains can be formed that are exactly equal in length to the length you have just made.

With 72 you would have the following: a line of 36 red rods

      „   „   „ 24 light green rods

---

* 4, 6, 8, 9, 10, 12, 14, 15, 16, 18, 20, 21, 24, 25, 27, 28, 30, 32, 35, 36, 40, 42, 45, 48, 49, 50, 54, 56, 60, 63, 64, 70, 72, 80, 81, 90, 100.

„   „   „ 18 pink rods

„   „   „ 12 dark green rods

„   „   „ 9 tan rods

„   „   „ 8 blue rods

More trains can be added if we use one or more orange rods in each factor with another rod end to end with it; so we can go on:

a line of   6 (orange + red)

„   „   „   4 (orange + tan)

„   „   „   3 (orange + orange + pink)

„   „   „   2 (orange + orange + orange + dark green)

If we set all this out in numerals we get:

$$72 = 2 \times 36 \text{ and } 36 \times 2$$
$$= 3 \times 24 \text{ and } 24 \times 3$$
$$= 4 \times 18 \text{ and } 18 \times 4$$
$$= 6 \times 12 \text{ and } 12 \times 6$$
$$= 8 \times 9 \text{ and } 9 \times 8$$

The factors of 72 are therefore: 2, 3, 4, 6, 8, 9, 12, 18, 24, 36.

The only crosses we can make with a pair of single rods are the tan/blue and blue/tan. But we can make crosses for each pair if we use more rods. Here are the other ones we can make:

red across (three orange and a dark green end to end)

light green across (two orange and a pink end to end)

pink across (an orange and tan end to end)

dark green across (an orange and red end to end).

So, altogether, we can make five crosses which, between them show all the ten factors of 72. We shall treat each cross as showing two products that are the reverse of each other. For example, 3 × 24 and 24 × 3 can be shown by the cross which has fight green across two orange and a pink end to end.

When we can form all the crosses for all the numbers on the 37 counters, we can play the following game:

3 Draw a counter and think of one product that is equal to that number. Check the answer.

When you have found one correct answer, write it down and form the cross. Look at the factors and see which can be halved (i.e. which rod can be replaced by two equal rods). If both can be halved, choose the larger. Form a new cross using the rod that is half the original one, but then double the other. Thus, if you drew 72 and made a cross with the product 8 × 9, your second cross would be 4 × 18. A third cross could be made with 2 × 36 (red over three orange and a dark green).

If you now fill in the rectangles and then place the rods end to end, you will always find you have the length, 72.

Do this with other numbers, making as many crosses as you can in this way, and see how many of them you now know.

4 For this game you need the cardboard materials. On the wall chart you will find only those factors that are not greater than 10. For 72, you find only 8 × 9, though you know there are many more.

Look at the wall chart and see how many you can recognize at once, naming the product and the number. The red/red sign stands for the red/red cross which you know gives the length of 4. Even if you did not know this, you could find it out by using the rods. Check any products of which you are not sure with your rods and find the number belonging to any signs you do not recognize.

You will notice that on the wall chart the signs are in groups. Take the first line and start with the tan/tan sign. If you halve a tan rod you get a pink rod and the pink/tan cross corresponds to half the tan/tan one. Halve the pink rod and you get the red rod. But you could have halved the other tan rod to get a pink/pink cross and the rectangles you can form from these two crosses are equivalent, as the trains made from them are equal in length. That is why both pair of products appear in this sign, giving four colored crescents instead of only two.

Taking the next sign to the left we see that the pink replaces the tan again and, in the last sign on the left, the pink has again been changed to red.

So, we have found all the crosses that can be formed if we begin with the tan/tan cross and proceed by halving. When we did this before, we doubled the second factor each time we halved the first one, so that the product itself did not change its value but, on the wall chart, we have simply halved one factor each time so that the product, and the number it yields, is halved repeatedly.

If we go from left to right, we find we are doubling each time. Thus, the first line gives us,

$2 \times 2 = 4 \quad 2 \times 4 = 8 \quad 2 \times 8 = 16 = 4 \times 4 \quad 4 \times 8 = 32 \quad 8 \times 8 = 64$

We know, also, though this does not appear on the chart, that $2 \times 16 = 32$ and that $4 \times 16 = 64 = 2 \times 32$.

You will now begin to understand why the other lines of the chart are arranged as they are. If you start on the left you are doubling when you move to the next one and if you start on the right you are halving; and you notice that one or other of the factors is doubled or halved each time as compared with the previous sign.

If you go through the counters you will find some that are the double, and some that are the double of the double, of others.

Find the number (or numbers) linked in that way with the following:

15   21   45   14   27

You can use the chart to help you, and the counters that represent the linked products can be placed beside the ones with which you began and with which they are connected.

The Product Cards

These provide a number of interesting games which can be played using only the products known, or with the whole pack.

The cards are shuffled and dealt to two players. They hold their cards so that they see all the signs. The object of the game is to obtain tricks consisting of two cards, and these are won by playing a product card whose value is bigger than that of the card played by the opponent.

The players, in turn, lay down a card which they hope will win the trick. The opponent looks for a card with a larger number and plays it if he thinks this is wise. If he has no card that will take the trick he will, of course, get rid of one with a small number.

You can become skilful at playing by practice. Here is an example of what can happen. If one player has products with the numbers 6, 18 and 72, and the other has the numbers 4, 24, and

56, the first may play 72 and win the trick but his opponent will play 4, and so can win the other two tricks.

Scoring is done by crediting each player with the value of the products in the tricks he has won. The player with the highest score wins.

Partners can play as well as single players.

The Bingo Game

This can be played by a number of players up to 10. In each case one player is banker and the others make their Bingo cards, according to the number of players using cards on the trays provided for this game.

The banker draws a counter and either calls its number or places it on the table. The players immediately try to find the sign to which the number belongs. The best way is to scan the card from left to right along the first line and then back from right to left for the second line, and so on downwards. The product shown on each sign, and the number made by those factors, should be repeated silently until the number needed is located.

The winner is the first player — or team — to have all the central circles on their set filled with the correct numbers.

If the players claim a number which belongs to their set but fail to connect it with the right sign, the counter is forfeited, and is placed on one side. This is also done if the players fail to claim a counter which they should have claimed.

This game is to be played using only those counters whose corresponding factors are known to the players, the rest of the counters being added as they become known. In this case the winner is the one who obtains the most counters when all have been played.

With all these multiplication games — and there are others you can make up, using the rods and the cardboard materials — you soon find that you know all your products perfectly and you will also discover many interesting relations between them.

In Books 1 and 2 of *Gattegno Mathematics*, the reader will find all the necessary set of exercises that will give the acquired knowledge its widest range. Tests are found in the workbooks 1-6 which cover the initial stages of this experience.

4 Johnny's Homework

Almost every day Johnny comes home from school with some new problem to solve. His homework contains so many different types of questions, according to the stage he has reached, that we cannot look at them all; but we can consider enough to give him the ideas he needs to cope with the rest.

1 Problems that Involve Only New Names

If Johnny can make his pattern of ten, using the orange rod, he knows he can write it down in the following way:

$$10 = 9 + 1 = 1 + 9 = 8 + 2 = 2 + 8 = 7 + 3 = 3 + 7 = 6 + 4 = 4 + 6 = 5 + 5$$

$$10 = 2 \times 4 + 2 \qquad 10 = 3 \times 3 + 1 \qquad 10 = 2 \times 5$$

$$10 = 4 \times 2 + 2 \qquad\qquad\qquad 10 = 5 \times 2$$

$$10 \div 4 = 2 \text{ r. } 2 \qquad 10 \div 3 = 3 \text{ r. } 1 \qquad 10 \div 2 = 5 \text{ r. } 0$$

$$10 \div 2 = 4 \text{ r. } 2 \qquad\qquad\qquad 10 \div 5 = 2 \text{ r. } 0$$

$$\tfrac{1}{2} \times 10 = 5 \qquad\qquad \tfrac{1}{5} \times 10 = 2 \qquad\qquad \tfrac{2}{5} \times 10 = 4$$

$$\tfrac{3}{5} \times 10 = 6 \qquad\qquad\qquad\qquad\qquad \tfrac{4}{5} \times 10 = 8$$

But what he knows perfectly well in this form can be presented to him in words that hide the answer he would otherwise give at once. Here are some examples:

1 If you have ten candies and give away three, how many have you left for yourself?

2 If you have six stamps and are given four more, and then give five to your brother, how many have you still got?

3 Can you share ten marbles equally among four boys? What will happen if you try to do so? How many will each boy get, and how many will be left over?

4 If I keep two-fifths of the ten equal coins I have in my pocket and share equally the rest amongst three friends, how many coins will each friend receive?

Johnny already knows the answers to these questions, and the fact that they are put in 'story' form does not make the answers any more difficult to find. He can become used to questions of this sort by playing a game he will enjoy.

He can begin with the rods and the written numerals that set out what they show, and then make up his own problems. The examples given above contain only a few of the possibilities and Johnny can make up all manner of fascinating problems of his own. If he plays with a friend, they can exchange the problems they have made and find the answers. Many of the stories they make up are likely to be about buying and selling, and it will not matter whether the money is in dollars, sterling, rupees or any other currency with which they are familiar. Wherever Johnny lives, he will find in the patterns of rods the kind of problem stories he gets at school, as well as the answers.

In this book we shall be using American money and the kind of story that American schoolchildren are familiar with but, as the arithmetic remains the same in every part of the world, the words can be changed without altering what is being done.

When Johnny is quite clear about how to use the pattern of ten he can work with larger numbers and he can make up thousands of stories and, by doing this for fun, he will learn to use words to illustrate the arithmetic he knows. The problems he thinks out for himself will be like the ones the textbook writers set him to solve, and he will no longer be baffled by problems put in word-form.

Here is a part of the pattern of twenty that can be used to make up story-problems:

$20 = 2 \times 10 = 2 \times 9 + 2 = 2 \times 8 + 4 = 3 \times 6 + 2 = 4 \times 5 = 5 \times 4 = 6 \times 3 + 2 = 10 \times 2$

$20 = 17 + 3 = 11 + 9 = 13 + 7 = 6 + 14 = 15 + 5 \ldots$

$20 = 1 + 2 + 3 + 4 + 10 = 6 + 4 + 3 + 7 \ldots$

And here are a few stories that Johnny might have thought out:

1   If we form rows of boys with six in each row, how many rows can we form with twenty boys? Will it be possible to see that every boy is in one of the rows?

And if we put only three boys in each row, how many rows shall we have? Will there be any boys left out?

2   If twenty sailors are marching in ranks, in how many ways can we arrange them so that each of the ranks contains the same number of sailors? Which arrangement gives the longest ranks, and which the shortest?

3   If I place one button on the table, two below this one, then three below the two, and so on, forming a triangle of buttons, how many rows will I make if I have only 20 buttons? Will I have any buttons left over? What will happen if I have 21 buttons?

4   There are twenty days left until the end of the term. Five of these days will be occupied by end-of-term tests. How many days will be left for lessons?

5   A week has seven days. How many weeks are there in twenty days? How many extra days would we need to make one more complete week?

6 Share twenty sheets of paper amongst three pairs of children in such a way that two of the pairs each have one more sheet than the third pair.

7 After spending half my money, I spend one fifth of what is left and I still have eight dollars. How many dollars did I have at first?

These questions are all easily solved with the rods. Take the last one, for instance. The tan rod is left after spending a fifth of half of what I had. Johnny knows that the tan is four-fifths of the orange rod, and he had twice that to begin with. So he had twenty dollars.

Orange	Red	Tan

If we take any school arithmetic book and look at any of the problems in it, we will see that it is simple compared with the ones we can invent with the rods. But the ones we make up are more fun because we can look at our rods and imagine they are people, cents, dollars, bottles, marbles or anything else we wish. There are so many story-problems waiting to be made up that no book, however thick, could contain them all; but we can find as many as we want in our own heads.

Let Johnny make a table of thirty-five and he will find many more stories to invent.

2 Sharing in Proportion

Here is a game that Johnny can easily play but which will later enable him to solve many difficult problems.

1 We begin by taking a red and a yellow rod which, end to end, equal the black. We see that the red is $\frac{2}{5}$ of the yellow and that the yellow is $\frac{5}{2}$ (or $2\frac{1}{2}$) of the red. When Johnny understands this, he can tackle such questions as these:

If we have 7 nuts, can we share them between two boys so that one has $\frac{2}{5}$ of what the other has?

Johnny will see that the answer is to give 2 nuts to one and 5 to the other.

If we had 14 nuts to be shared in the same way, what would the shares then be?

Johnny finds no difficulty, for with twice as many nuts to share each would get twice what he did before but the proportion will still be 2 nuts for the first to every 5 nuts for the second.

What if there were 21 nuts or 28 nuts, and the shares were to be in the same proportion?

2   We now take the length of 9, using any two rods to form it, and share 9 nuts, first in the proportion of the two rods we have chosen.

52

Let Johnny then find the answers when the number of nuts to be shared in that proportion is a multiple of 9, say, 18, 63 or 108.

The rods used to make up the length of 9 can be changed so that the problems are changed, and we can then do the same with any length that can be formed with two complementary rods. In every case, the two rods chosen can be used to provide a proportion in which the total length can be shared, and we can use the rods and their number values to represent whatever it is we wish to share out. For example,

3   21 = 11 + 10. Can we share $63 between two people in the proportion of 11 to 10? Or $84? Or $147?

73 = 33 + 40. Can we share $7.30 between two people in the proportion of 33 to 40? Or $14.60? Or $146?

The answer to these questions is found each time by putting end to end two rods equal to the *terms of the proportion* (2 to 5, or 11 to 10, or 33 to 40) and comparing the given number with the length. If the given number, as in (Question 1), is 7 and the length is equal to 7 whites, the answer is simple. It is the value in white rods of each of the two composing rods. If, as in (Question 3), the given number is 147 and the length is 21 whites, we must find the number of times that 21 is contained in 147 (i.e. 7) and multiply the value of each of the rods by that number. 7 × 11 = 77 and 7 × 10 = 70, so one receives $77 and the other $70.

So, too, with the question in (Question 3) about dollars. If the lengths of 33 and 40 are placed end to end, we obtain 73. But 7.3

is $\frac{1}{10}$ of 73, so 33 and 40 must each be divided by 10, giving the answer \$3.30 and \$4.00. Sharing \$14.60 is done in the same way, for $14.6 = \frac{1}{5}$ of 73. We transform $\frac{1}{5}$ into its equivalent $\frac{2}{10}$ and multiply 33 and 40 by $\frac{2}{10}$, getting the answer \$6.60 and \$8.oo.

4   So far we have worked with whole numbers for the terms of the proportion, but we may wish to share a quantity, say 24, between two people in the proportion of $2\frac{1}{2}$ to $3\frac{1}{2}$. We can do this as follows:

Take the red rod as your unit so that the yellow rod represents $2\frac{1}{2}$ and the black rod $3\frac{1}{2}$. End to end the yellow and black equal 6 red rods. 6 is a quarter of 24. We should need 4 yellow and 4 black to make the length of 24, if these are to be given the values of $2\frac{1}{2}$ and $3\frac{1}{2}$ we chose for them. So we must multiply $2\frac{1}{2}$ and $3\frac{1}{2}$ by 4 to get our answer: $4 \times 2\frac{1}{2} = 10$ and $4 \times 3\frac{1}{2} = 14$. We must give 10 to one and 14 to the other.

But what if we wished to share 20 in that proportion, instead of 24. Can we still do it? Yes, because we can find how much 20 is of 24 (i.e. $\frac{20}{24} = \frac{5}{6}$) and multiply 10 and 14 by $\frac{5}{6}$. This gives $\frac{50}{6}$ or $8\frac{1}{3}$ and $\frac{70}{6} = 11\frac{2}{3}$

So we can divide any number into two parts proportionally in whole numbers or in fractions, and we can find an answer that must be expressed as a fraction.

What will help Johnny as he plays these games is to see that if he makes any length of rods, using so many of one color and so many of another, he can make up problems like the ones he finds in his own textbook. Here is another kind of story problem he can invent in this way:

5 Put 4 light green rods end to end with 2 yellow ones to make the length of 22 white ones. Johnny can use this to say:

"If I had $22 and wanted to share this sum of money among six people, so that four of them each get $\frac{3}{5}$ of what each of the other two get, how much will each receive?"

He sees that the answer is obvious because there are four rods each having the value 3, and two having the value 5.3 is $\frac{3}{5}$ of 5, so the four have each $\frac{3}{5}$ of what each of the other two receive.

Johnny can vary his problem to make it seem more difficult. He can make it $110 to be shared in the same way. He knows that 110 is 22 × 5 and that he must multiply 3 and 5 by 5 to get the new answer. 3 × 5 = 15 and 5 × 5 = 25, so four people will get $15 each and two will get $25 each.

To check, Johnny will work out that 4 × 15 = 60 and that 2 × 25 = 50. 60 + 50 = 110. He will then check that 15 to 25 is the same proportion as 3 to 5. He finds it is because $\frac{15}{25} = \frac{3}{5}$.

If Johnny has not yet mastered fractions he will soon be able to work happily with them and he can then tackle the games in which they are needed. Meanwhile, he can practice this game of making up problems and solving them himself, for instance using the following pairs of rods:

- red and black

- pink and yellow

- light green and tan.

At first he can take the total number of rods as the number of people amongst whom a sum of money is to be divided. The total length (using the white rod as the unit of measurement) will give the amount, and the two rods chosen will give the proportion in which the division is to be made.

Since he is not restricted to money questions, he can make up other problems using pounds of sugar, ices and candy or paint on windows and doors, choosing his proportions and his quantities as he pleases.

All these problems can be made easy by using the rods to represent any quantity and the number of them to correspond with the number amongst which the division is to be made. The only matter requiring thought is the choice of rods needed to give the proportion. Once suitable rods have been chosen in the correct number to represent the length, the working out of the answer is done exactly as above. Practice at making up such problems will enable Johnny to understand and solve the ones he is given at school.

3 Length, Area and Volume

All the problems that are concerned with rectangular figures become obvious when the rods are used, whether the rectangles are parts of plane or solid figures.

For instance, if we want to use a plot of land to build a house with a lawn and a path round it, and a flower garden and orchard, we can represent this by the choice of suitable rods. We could use white rods to represent the site of the house, green ones for the lawn, and red for the path. Here are two examples:

1 On a plot of land 30 ft. × 50 ft., we want to build a house with four equal sized rooms and a kitchen, bathroom and garage. We propose to have a front lawn with flower beds and a vegetable garden at the back, and paths. Use the rods to make the dimensions, starting, perhaps, with one white rod as a square foot or a yellow rod as representing 10 ft. for the making of the fence.

2 A model of a house can be made with white rods for the floor, and different rods for walls, windows, and doors.

Using plans or models like these, you can make up problems about the cost of building the house or fencing in the garden. Or you can calculate how many bricks you need, or how many bags of cement would be required to make a concrete floor. Then there are the doors and windows. How much wood will be needed and how much will it cost? How much glass for the panes?

There are so many models Johnny can make — blocks of flats with shops at street level and studios on top, or a fine staircase for a new town hall, a warehouse, swimming-pools with buildings all round, the plan of a church, or a model of one with pillars and a cross.

He should try to make his dimensions reasonable and, in working out quantities of materials and prices, he should try to find out what would be required in real life and how much it would cost.

If he knows how to calculate areas and volumes it will be much more interesting but, if not, he will be discovering about these later on in this book and can then use his knowledge for these games of construction.

The experience he gains will help him with the problems set at school because he will understand better what is involved in what he is doing and he will grasp what he is required to do and see how he can set about it.

Parts of Textbook 2 and all of Textbook 3 of *Gattegno Mathematics,* deal with problems about sharing, proportion, length, perimeter, area and volume as well as problems about grouping, cost price, selling price, money, capacity and weight.

5 Some More Mysteries Made Clear

In this chapter we shall play some more games with the rods (and sometimes with the product cards) that will leave us in no doubt that mathematics is fun at all levels.

1 Highest Common Factor (H.C.F.)

We already know how to make crosses to represent numbers that have factors. If we take two such numbers and make their crosses we shall sometimes find that both crosses have a particular rod in common.

Thus the crosses for 6 and 8 are red/light green and red/pink. We see that red is common to both, and we know that this is because 2 is a factor of both numbers, 2 × 3 and 2 × 4.3 is not common, nor is 4. We shall shorten *common factor* of two numbers into C.F.

Find the C.F. of 14 and 21, 18 and 27, 16 and 20.

With this last pair of numbers, we could have as our crosses 2 × 8 and 2 × 10, but we could equally have 4 × 4 and 4 × 5. So 2 and 4 are both common factors. We could have found all the factors of both numbers by making two towers of crossed rods using only the smallest rods possible. These towers would then have been 2 × 2 × 2 × 2 and 2 × 2 × 5 respectively. By looking at these we would have seen that 2 × 2 was common to both and we could have substituted for two red rods a pink rod in each, giving us 4 × 2 × 2 and 4 × 5. This would have shown us 4 as common factor.

2 and 4 are the only common factors we can find and, as 4 is a cross, therefore higher than 2, it is called the *highest common factor* of these two numbers and we write it H.C.F.

We can find the H.C.F. of two numbers by writing down in order all the factors that can be found in each, marking the ones that are common and choosing the largest. The factors can be found by dividing each number first by 2, then by 3, then by 4 and so on, writing down the numbers that go exactly into the given number.

For example, the factors of 24 and 36 are:

24: 2, 3, 4, 6, 8, 12

36: 2, 3, 4, 6, 9, 12, 18

The H.C.F. is 12.

If we had made towers of crossed rods, using the smallest possible rods or *prime factors* we should have had:

24: 2, 2, 2, 3

36: 2, 2,   3, 3

We have arranged the factors to show which are common, and we find two of 2 and one of 3. The top line has another 2, but it is not matched in the line below, and the bottom line has another 3 which is not matched in the line above. These are not common. If we multiply together the factors that *are* common we have $2 \times 2 \times 3 = 12$.

We could also have made crosses for the two numbers by treating orange and red end to end (i.e. 12) as a factor in the crosses and placing a red rod across the first and a light green rod across the second. Again we should have found 12 as the H.C.F. and we should notice that 2 and 3 remained as the non-common factors.

But the most striking way of showing the H.C.F. remains the crosses and towers because one actually sees that one of the common factors is a tower taller than all the others.

We could have included 1 and 24 as factors of 24, and 1 and 36 as factors of 36 because $1 \times 24 = 24$ and $1 \times 36 = 36$. But this would not have given us a common factor higher than 12. We should remember these special factors, however, as we shall see if we look for the H.C.F. of 12 and 36:

12: 1, 2, 3, 4, 6, 12

36: 1, 2, 3, 4, 6, 12, 18, 36

Here 12 is the H.C.F. of these two numbers.

We have seen several ways in which we can find the H.C.F. of two numbers but, whichever we choose, we are either finding *all* the factors for each and choosing the highest common one, or we are finding all the *prime* factors for each, choosing the common ones and multiplying them together. We can see from the rods why both ways of doing it are correct and why they give us the highest factor that will go exactly into both numbers.

Use both methods (and the rods) to find the H.C.F. of: 6 and 9, 13 and 26, 20 and 28, 21 and 33.

When we wish to express in writing what the H.C.F. of two numbers is, we use brackets like these:

$$(12, 36) = 12$$

But (24, 36) = 12, and (12, 48) = 12. So one number may be the H.C.F. of different pairs.

Two numbers may have 1 as their H.C.F. For example, (5, 7) = 1, and (7, 12) = 1, and (10, 21) = 1. There is no common factor of any of these pairs that is higher than 1.

When this is so, we say that the two numbers are *relatively prime,* but this does not mean that the numbers must themselves be prime; they are prime only with respect to each other.

(5, 7) = 1.   5 and 7 are both prime numbers.

(7, 12) = 1.   7 is prime but 12 is not. 12 is, however, prime with respect to 7.

(10, 21) = 1.   Here, neither number is prime but each is prime relatively to the other.

A prime number is prime with respect to all other numbers. It has no factors apart from 1 and itself. With the rods, we can find which numbers are prime numbers by seeing whether, when we have formed that number using the appropriate rod or rods end to end, we can make up that length with a train of rods of any single color. If we cannot, the number is prime.

If we look for the H.C.F. of a number with respect to itself, the answer is that same number. So (7, 7) = 7 and (3, 3) = 3.

If we look for the H.C.F. of a number and *any* of its multiples, that number is the answer. So, (12, 12) = 12, (12, 24) = 12, (12, 36) = 12 and (12, 48) = 12 and so on.

We need not restrict ourselves to finding the H.C.F. for two numbers only. Let us take three, say, 12, 15 and 18. We make their crosses and find their factors:

12: 1, 2, 3, 4,   6,   12

15: 1,   3,   5,   15

18: 1, 2, 3,   6,   9,   18

We find that 1 and 3 are common to all. 2 is common to only two, and so is 6, so 3 is the highest common factor.

(12, 15, 18) = 3.

We can take more than 3 numbers, say 14, 21, 35, 42 and 49 and, by finding their factors and choosing the highest, we obtain their H.C.F.:

14: 1, 2,   7,   14

21: 1,   3,   7,   21

35: 1,   5, 7,   35

42: 1, 2, 3,   6,   7,   14,   21,   42

49: 1,   7,   49

7 is the H.C.F. or (14, 21, 35, 42, 49) = 7.

Let Johnny find for himself the H.C.F. of

(9, 21)   (15, 25)   (14, 34)   (16, 24, 56)

2 Lowest Common Multiple (L.C.M.)

In Chapter II we played games with trains and we shall now play some more to see what else we can learn from them.

Let us make a long red train and a long light green one, placing them side by side, taking care to see that they are exactly the same length. The rods can be thought of as coaches.

We see that we could uncouple coaches at several points to make smaller trains which would also be equal in length. The shortest we could make would have 2 light green coaches and 3 red ones, which are both the length of a dark green rod or 6.

Let us try this with a black train and a yellow one side by side. We can find equal lengths with 5 black and 7 yellow, with 10 black and 14 yellow, and with 15 black and 21 yellow coaches. If we went on, and had enough rods, we could make as many as we wished, but the *shortest* we can make has the length of 3 orange rods with 1 yellow added, so it has the length 35.

Repeat this with black and tan and with pink and blue rods, finding the shortest equal trains and measuring that length.

Here are some of the trains we have made, with some others we have not made, described in writing:

light green and red

$3 + 3$ $+ 3 + 3$ $+ 3 + 3$ $+ 3 + 3$ $+ 3 + 3$ ...

$2 + 2 + 2$ $+ 2 + 2 + 2$ $+ 2 + 2 + 2$ $+ 2 + 2 + 2$ $+ 2 + 2 + 2$ ...

The shortest train is 2×3 or $3 \times 2 = 6$.

black and yellow

$7 + 7 + 7 + 7 + 7$ $+ 7 + 7 + 7 + 7 + 7$ $\cdot \cdot \cdot$

$5 + 5 + 5 + 5 + 5 + 5 + 5$ $+ 5 + 5 + 5 + 5 + 5 + 5 + 5$ ...

The shortest train is 5×7 or $7 \times 5 = 35$.

Let us now make a dark green train side by side with a tan train. For this we get:

6 + 6 + 6 + 6   + 6 + 6 + 6 + 6   + 6 + 6 + 6 + 6 . . .

8 + 8 + 8   + 8 + 8 + 8   + 8 + 8 + 8 . . .

Here, for our shortest equal trains we have, 4x6 or 3 x8=24.

With a blue train and a light green we get:

3 + 3 + 3   + 3 + 3 + 3   + 3 + 3 + 3   + 3 + 3 + 3   . . .

9   + 9   + 9   + 9   . . .

The shortest is 3×3 or $1 \times 9 = 9$.

We could go on making such trains and finding the shortest sections of them that form equal trains, remembering always that all the coaches in each train must be rods of the same color.

If we look at the lengths of all the equal trains we have formed, whether they are the shortest or not, we notice that each length is a *multiple* of the length of the carriages that make it up. Thus, in the first train we made, 6 is a multiple of both 2 and 3. In the second, 35 is a multiple of both 5 and 7. In the dark green and tan trains, 24 is a multiple of both 6 and 8, and, in the last, 9 is a multiple of both 3 and 9.

We find the same is true if we measure the longer sections of these pairs that are equal but we have chosen the shortest each time, and so we have found the *least common multiple* of lengths of the coaches. In the first we say that 6 is the least common multiple (or L.C.M.) of 2 and 3, and in the last that 9 is the L.C.M. of 3 and 9. In fact we have been finding the L.C.M. of all these pairs of numbers, represented by the different colored rods, by finding the shortest trains of equal length that we could form with those rods.

Look again at the red and light green trains. We found equal sections of coaches at 6, 12, 18, 24, 30 . . . With the black and yellow trains we found our equal sections at 35 and 70 and we could have gone on to find them at 105, 140 . . .

In both these cases, we notice that the shortest length is found to be equal to the two numbers multiplied together: $2 \times 3 = 6$ and $5 \times 7 = 35$. But, with the dark green and tan trains we found that the L.C.M. was 24 which is only half of 6×8. We find a similar result with the light green and blue trains, the L.C.M. of which is 9 and not 3×9.

So the L.C.M. is the product of the numbers themselves only if those numbers are relatively prime, that is to say, if they have no common factor.

To find the L.C.M. of numbers that have a common factor we first find their H.C.F. and then multiply it by the factors that are not common. We shall take 6 and 8 as an example:

6: 1, 2, 3,   6   or 6 = 2 × 3

8: 1, 2,   4,   8   or 8 = 2 × 4

If we take a multiple of 2, 3 and 4, the number we obtain will be a multiple of both 6 and 8 because every multiple of 2 and 3 is a multiple of 6 and every multiple of 2 and 4 is a multiple of 8.

2 × 3 × 4 is the smallest such multiple, so 24 is the L.C.M. of 6 and 8. This agrees with what we found with the rods.

Now let us take 3 and 9 as an example:

3: 1,   3   or 3 = 3 × 1

9: 1,   3,   9   or 9 = 3 × 3 × 1

If we take a multiple of 1, 3, and 3, it will be a multiple of both 3 and 9 because every multiple of 1 and 3 is a multiple of 3, and every multiple of 3 and 3 is a multiple of 9. But 1 × 3 × 3 is the smallest such multiple, so 9 is the L.C.M. of 3 and 9. This is what we have already discovered with the rods.

We write [2, 3] for 'the L.C.M. of 2 and 3,' so we can write, [2, 3] = 6. You will, accordingly, know what is meant by the writing:

[6, 8] = 24   [7, 5] = 35

[5, 7] = 35   [3, 9] = 9

We can find the L.C.M. of more than two numbers because, instead of having only two one-color trains side by side, we can have three, four, or more, and we can still find the shortest length at which they are all equal. This, we can see, is the L.C.M. of the lengths of their coaches.

Let Johnny try this with three long trains, one yellow, one light green and one red:

Yellow train:	6 coaches	6 coaches	6 coaches
Light green train:	10 ,,	10 ,,	10 ,,
Red train:	15 ,,	15 ,,	15 ,,

The lengths at which the three trains are equal are 30, 60, 90 . . . (using the white rod to measure). The shortest of these is 30, so the L.C.M. of 2, 3 and 5 is 30, or [2, 3, 5] = 30.

Let him take light green, yellow and black trains side by side and find the L.C.M. of 3, 5 and 7.

If the light green train is replaced by the dark green, what is the length of the shortest train?

Instead of choosing numbers that are relatively prime, as we have been doing, we can take three that have a common factor, say, light green, dark green and blue and find the shortest equal trains, and do it again with pink, dark green and orange.

If we had chosen dark green, tan and orange rods we should find 2 as their H.C.F. and 3, 4 and 5 as the non-common factors. We already know that the L.C.M. of 3, 4 and 5 is 3 × 4 × 5, i.e. 60. So the L.C.M. of 6, 8, 10 is 120. Or [6, 8, 10] = 120.

We can now find, for example, the L.C.M. of 6, 7, 8

2, 5, 7

2, 4, 6

3, 4, 12

3 Series

If we make a staircase with one of each of the ten rods, as we have done before, and then make another in reverse order, the two staircases will fit together to form a rectangle with eleven lines which we can read in numerals as follows:

10, 9 + 1, 8 + 2, 7 + 3, 6 + 4, 5 + 5, 4 + 6, 3 + 7, 2 + 8, 1 + 9, 10

Each line would need ten white rods to cover it and, as there are eleven lines, we should require 10 × 11 to cover the whole rectangle. So, to cover one staircase we should need half that number.

$$\frac{10 \times 11}{2} = 55$$

This is the length that would be made by the white rods if they were placed end-to-end. In numerals,

$$1 + 2 + 3 + 4 + 5 + 6 + 7 + 8 + 9 + 10 = 55$$

But we could have formed a slightly different rectangle if we had fitted the staircases together so that the first and last lines were each made up by an orange and white rod. If we do this we have ten lines, but each now has a length of 11. Once again we should require $11 \times 10 = 110$ white rods to cover it and 55 to cover each staircase. In numerals,

$$10 + 1, 9 + 2, 8 + 3, 7 + 4, 6 + 5, 5 + 6, 4 + 7, 3 + 8, 2 + 9, 1 + 10$$

If we now remove the two white rods, we can form a new rectangle, the first and last lines of which will be composed of an orange and red rod. The length of all the lines will be 12, and there will be nine fines. $12 \times 9 = 108$, $108 \div 2 = 54$. The sum of the series 2 to 10 is, thus, 54, which we could have foreseen.

Let us remove the two red rods as well, and form another rectangle in the same way. We will expect to get the answer 52. Let us check whether we do, and then try again, after removing the fight green rods, observing whether we get the result we would expect.

We can make use of the series 1, 2, 3 . . . 10 with which we began to make a series of different type, in which the steps are not equal but increase in a regular manner. If we go up through the series stopping at each step to add the terms to give us the next step, we get a series like this:

1

1 + 2

1 + 2 + 3

1 + 2 + 3 + 4

which we can continue up to,

1 + 2 + 3 + 4 + 5 + 6 + 7 + 8 + 9 + 10.

If we do the additions we find we have a series 1, 3, 6, 10, 15 . . . 55, which we could continue further if we wished.

If we move up by using a red or light green rod instead of a white one we find new series:

1   1

1 + 2   1 + 3

$1 + 2 + 4$	or	$1 + 3 + 6$
$1 + 2 + 4 + 6$		$1 + 3 + 6 + 9$
$1 + 2 + 4 + 6 + 8$		$1 + 3 + 6 + 9 + 12$
$1 + 2 + 4 + 6 + 8 + 10$		$1 + 3 + 6 + 9 + 12 + 15$

We could, of course, use a pink rod in the same way, or any other rod or length we care to choose, and there is no need to stop at any point, because we can always see how to form the next step.

Let Johnny add more lines to the series above and form new series of his own and do the additions to see what the series looks like.

Now let us return to the series that begins with 1 and move upwards by equal steps. The one with which we began increased by 1 each time. In staircases that go up by 2 each time, or 3, let us complete the rectangle by fitting a second staircase in reverse, as we did before, and see how many white rods are needed to cover it.

For example, if the series is (in numerals) 1, 4, 7, 10, 13 we find a rectangle of sides 14 and 5. $14 \times 5 = 70$, so 70 whites are needed in order to cover it and 35 to cover each staircase. So, $1 + 4 + 7 + 10 + 13 = 35$. On checking, this is found to be correct.

This is interesting because it means that, when we have a long addition of that sort, we do not need to add all the terms. We can use what we have discovered to find the answer rapidly.

Suppose for example, we wish to add $1 + 5 + 9 + 13 \ldots 41$. If we made a staircase for this series and fitted a second one to it, we should obtain a rectangle that we can indicate by the numerals set out below:

$$1 + 41$$

$$5 + 37$$

$$9 + 33$$

$$13 + 29$$

$$17 + 25$$

$$21 + 21$$

$$25 + 17$$

$$29 + 13$$

$$33 + 9$$

$$37 + 5$$

$$41 + 1$$

The rectangle would have eleven lines, each 42 in length. $11 \times 42 = 462$. $\frac{1}{2} \times 42 \times 11 = 21 \times 11 = 231$. This takes less time than adding up the eleven terms from 1 to 41.

The example given can be used to test series that do not begin at 1. If we take the series from, say, 13 to 37, there would be seven lines (or terms) of 50. $\frac{1}{2} \times 50 \times 7 = 25 \times 7 = 175$. Is this correct?

We can, however, look at series that do not begin with 1 in a different way.

We see below the first steps of a series that begins at 3 and increases by 2 at each step.

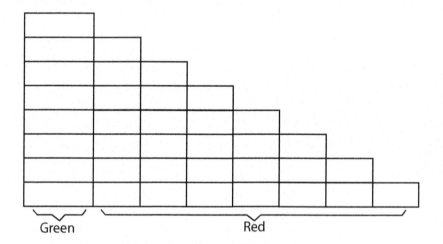

Green   Red

If we use the rods to make this series and continue until there are 12 light green rods (with the correct number of red ones needed to form the appropriate lengths), how many steps will there be in the staircase? And what is the length of the longest line?

We can make another such staircase in reverse and fit it to the first to form a rectangle. It will have green rods at each end and red ones between. It is easy to find the number of white rods needed to cover this rectangle, and it would require half that number to cover the staircase. End to end these white rods would equal the length of the terms (or steps) in the series. The figure below is, of course, intended only to illustrate what is being done; it does not contain as many lines as the one you have made with the rods.

We can see from the rods that the *successive* steps are

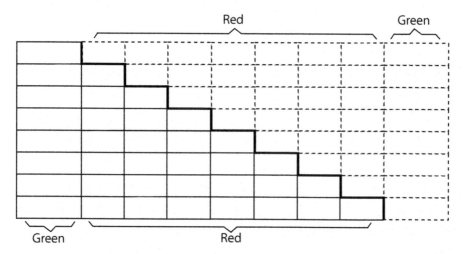

1 light green; 1 light green + 1 red; 1 light green + 2 red and so on up to 1 light green + 11 red rods. If we use *g* for light green and *r* for red, we can write,

$$g + (g + r) + (g + 2r) + (g + 3r) + \ldots (g + 11r)$$

From this we can see how many red rods there are in each step.

The 1st step has no red rods

The 2nd step has 1 red rod

The 3rd step has 2 red rods

The 4th step has 3 red rods and so on.

If we were asked how many red rods there would be in the 7th step or the 12th we could answer immediately without counting the rods.

The second staircase which we fitted to the first is in reverse and we should read it as follows:

$$(g + 11r) + (g + 10r) + (g + 9r) \ldots + (g + 3r) + (g + 2r) + (g + r) + g$$

Looking at the rectangle we see 12 green rods forming a line at each end and eleven lines containing 12 red rods each. The whole rectangle would be,

$12 \times (2g + 11r)$ which we can write also as $12[g + (g + 11r)]$. Each staircase will require half that number:

$$\frac{12}{2} \times [g + (g + 11r)].$$

So, if we know the first term of a series, the step by which its terms increase, and the number of its terms, we can find the sum of the terms of the series without needing to add them.

We try other examples by simply changing the number of steps and replacing the light green rod and the red rods by rods of other colors. In this way we can make series of our own with elements *we* have chosen; then find the number of white rods needed to cover the staircase by forming the rectangle with a second staircase as before. We can forecast the answer by using the *formula* we have just found and changing the letters and numerals to agree with the choice of rods we have made and the number of the terms (or steps) we decided to have.

The staircases we have been playing with are called arithmetical series and, in them, only the sign + is used (though × is found in the formula). In the next section we shall find series of another type called geometric in which only the sign × is used.

4 Towers and Powers[*]

If we take a yellow rod and place another across it, a cross is formed which we shall write as $y \times y$. If we take a third and lay it across the top, we have a 'tower' which we can write as $y \times y \times y$. By using more yellow rods in the same way, going as high as we like we make a tower that can be read as $y \times y \times y \times y \times y \times y \times y \times y$

We can make other similar towers with red rods and with black rods, and see what height these towers are by counting the rods.

---

[*] Cf. Gattegno Mathematics Books 2, 5, 7 for addition examples and uses. Some diagrams in these books could also be of assistance to the readers or the children.

For the yellow tower with 8 rods we write y^8. This will tell us at once which rod we used and the height of the tower we made.

What would these mean: y^3, y^5, y^9?

What would r^6, r^1, r^4, r^{10} mean, if r stands for the red rod?

What would b^2, b^7, b^{10} mean, if b stands for the black rod?

The way to read what we have written down is: y^5 is *y to the 5th power* (or simply '*to the fifth*'). So r^7 would be *r* to the 7th power or to the seventh.

All the expressions we have written for the towers we have made can be read as powers of y, or r, or b, or B, or t.

When making the yellow tower we *multiplied* by y each time we placed a rod across another. With the blue tower we were multiplying by B each time. As each successive rod was introduced the small figure which gave us the power had to be increased by 1. This figure is called the *index*.

If we remove a rod from a tower the index is reduced by 1, and we divide by y or r or whatever rod it happened to be.

If we take a tower representing r^3 and another representing r^4, and place one on top of the other to make a single red tower: how high is the new tower? And how would we express it in writing? What we have done was to multiply r^3 by r^4 or r^4 by r^3, but when we write this down with the answer we find it is:

$$r^3 \times r^4 = r^7.$$

Let us find the answer to the following, using rods if we are not sure, and also to check:

$$y^2 \times y^7, \qquad y^1 \times y^4, \qquad y^3 \times y^4, \qquad y^2 \times y^6, \qquad y^2 \times y^3$$

$$b^2 \times b^4 \qquad b^4 \times b^2, \qquad b^3 \times b^3, \qquad b^1 \times b^5 \qquad b^5 \times b^1$$

$$r^1 \times r^9 \qquad r^9 \times r^1 \qquad r^7 \times r^3, \qquad r^3 \times r^7 \qquad r^2 \times r^8$$

$$r^5 \times r^5 \qquad r^4 \times r^6 \qquad r^6 \times r^4, \qquad r^6 \times r^4 \qquad r^1 \times r^1$$

We could, of course, put three or more towers on top of each other to make higher ones:

$$y^2 \times v^2 \times y^2 \quad \textit{or} \quad y^2 \times y^3 \times v^2 \quad \textit{or} \quad y^3 \times y^3 \times y^3$$

Two of the powers we have met have special names.

y^2, r^2 and b^2 are called *squares* and y^3, r^3 and b^3 are called *cubes*. When we use the term 'square' in this way we mean that the rod in question is multiplied by itself. So $y \times y$ is y^2, or y squared, or y to the second power, $y^5 \times y^5$ is *the square of y to the fifth*, and we know that its value is y to the tenth.

So, too, $b^3 \times b^3$ is the *square of b cubed*. The term cube means here, that the number is multiplied by itself and then multiplied again by itself. $y^3 \times y^3 \times y^3$ is the *cube of y cubed*.

Let us practice reading the following:

$$b^7 \times b^7, \quad p^4 \times p^4 \times p^4, \quad r^6 \times r^6, \quad r^9 \times r^9 \times r^9$$

$$t^2 \times t^2, \quad g^8 \times g^8 \times g^8, \quad r^1 \times r^1, \quad y^6 \times y^6 \times y^6$$

Here is a game in which the question sounds amusing and the answer can be found with the rods. *Is the square of the cube different from the cube of the square?* We can use yellow rods or red rods for the tower, and use this knowledge to compare,

$$(y^2)^3 \text{ or } y^2 \times y^2 \times y^2 \text{ with } (y^3)^2 \text{ or } y^3 \times y^3$$

and, $(r^4)^3$ or $r^4 \times r^4 \times r^4$ with $(r^3)^4$ or $r^3 \times r^3 \times r^3 \times r^3$

Can we find the height of a tower made in the following way:

$$r^5 \times r^7, \quad b^4 \times b^2 \times b^6, \quad c^5 \times c^5 \times c^2 \times c^2 \quad c^7 \times c^7$$

$$(b^3)^4 \quad (b^4)^3 \quad (t^6)^2 \quad (B^2)^5$$

Find it first without the rods, using what you have learned so far, and then check with the rods.

When we increased the number of rods we multiplied and, when we removed some we divided. So, to get y^4 from y^7 we divided by y^3.

This can be written in two ways.

$$y^7 \div y^4 = y^3 \text{ or } \frac{y^7}{y^4} = y^3$$

Let Johnny make towers and find the answer to,

$$y^9 \div y^2, \quad y^5 \div y^3, \quad y^7 \div y^5, \quad y^8 \div y^7, \quad y^{10} \div y^6,$$

$$\frac{r^6}{r^4}, \frac{r^7}{r^9}, \frac{r^4}{r^9}, \frac{r^5}{r^4}, \frac{r^{10}}{r^8}$$

We can mix the two processes of introducing and removing rods and we can do this in any order, and find the answers to:

$$\frac{r^4 \times r^2}{r^3}, \quad \frac{r^6 \times r^2}{r^3}, \quad \frac{r^5 \times r^5}{r^6}, \quad \frac{r^7 \times r^9}{r^{10}}$$

One more game with powers can be added without meeting any new difficulty.

We can begin with a yellow rod and put red rods, one by one, across to make a tower as high as we like. This will give us the successive steps:

$$y, \quad y \times r, \quad y \times r \times r, \quad y \times r \times r \times r, \quad y \times r \times r \times r \times r, \ldots$$

or, $\quad y, \quad y \times r^1, \quad y \times r^2, \quad y \times r^3, \quad y \times r^4, \quad y \times r^5, \ldots$

The first term has *no* red rods

The second term has r^1 in it,

The third term has $\quad r^2$ in it,

The fourth term has $\quad r^3$ in it,

The fifth term has $\quad r^4$ in it and so on.

If we were asked to give the expression of the 9th, 11th, or 15th term, or any other, we could do so. We have already met the same kind of situation in the arithmetical series in which we began with a light green rod and increased the length at each step by a red rod, but this is an example of a geometric series in which the only sign used is ×.

Notice that the first term could be written $y \times 1$ and, as it has no red rod across it, we could say it has o red rods and write $y \times r^o$. This would be for the sake of uniformity only, because r^o means nothing real, and no one can say what it is as an operation. But because it can be written, and can replace the 1 in $y \times 1$, people use it. So we can keep in mind that r^o is always equal to 1 so long as r denotes a number by which we *can* multiply. Again, $r^o = 1$ is only a way of writing. b^o or g^o or y^o are also only ways of writing, and each can be replaced by 1 or can replace 1 in written statements.

5 Squares

With the rods we can make many squares — red, light green, pink, and so on up to orange. We can compare each square with the others. If we look at the white rod we see that it is a cube and that each of its faces is a square, the sides of each such square being 1 cm.

If we measure only the sides of each of the squares from the white one to the orange one, using the white as the unit, we find they are:

1 cm. 2 cm. 3 cm. 4 cm. 5 cm. 6 cm. 7 cm. 8 cm. 9 cm. 10 cm.

If we measure the *areas* of these squares, using the white square as the unit, we get:

1 sq. cm., 4 sq. cm., 9 sq. cm., 16 sq. cm., and so on up to 100 sq. cm.

Of course it would take too long to place white rods on the squares and to count them, and we can find the area rapidly by mental multiplication. Thus, the black square has seven rods side by side and each of them would require seven white rods to cover its whole length. So, to cover the seven black would require 7×7, i.e. 49 white rods.

We can play amusing and instructive games with squares.

Let us make a red square, a light green square, and a yellow square, placing them as shown in the figure.

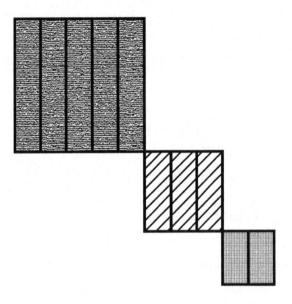

How does this figure compare in area with the orange square? We have chosen the orange square because a red, a green and a yellow rod end to end form the length of the orange rod.

We can obtain the answer by mental multiplication, but we can find a more satisfying answer if we study the rods and ask ourselves, first, how we can compare the red and green squares with the yellow one. This is a similar question because we know that the red and green rods end to end make up the length of the yellow one.

If we place the red and green squares on top of the yellow one, as shown in the next figure, we see that the yellow square is greater than the *sum* of the red and green squares; but by looking at the yellow left uncovered, we can see by how much it is greater. We see two yellow rectangles left uncovered and the dimensions of both are the same.

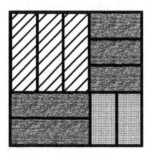

Two green rods side by side will cover each exactly, and so will three red ones. So the difference between the yellow square and the sum of the red and green squares is equal to two equal rectangles whose sides are the same length as the sides of the two smaller squares. (By 'sum' we mean that the areas of the squares are added together. So the rods they contain, if laid end to end, would give us the sum.)

We can try this, using different squares, for example:

1 black, light green and pink

2 tan, red and dark green

3 orange, light green and black.

Now that we know what the word 'sum' means, we can put what we have found in the following language: *The sum of the squares is less than the square of the sum,* or, *the square of the sum is greater than the sum of the squares.*

As we have seen, we can also know by how much the square of the sum is greater than the sum of the squares. It is greater by two equal rectangles with sides which are the lengths of the sides of the smaller squares.

Let us put this in a mysterious way, using the letter code set out below:

w = white	d = dark green
r = red	b = black
g = light green	t = tan
p = pink	B = blue
y = yellow	o = orange

To express the squares formed with the rods we shall write w^2, r^2, g^2, p^2 and so on up to o^2.

Can we see why the following statements are true?

$$O^2 = g^2 + b^2 + 2 \times g \times b \qquad B^2 = p^2 + y^2 + 2 \times p \times y$$

$$b^2 = r^2 + y^2 + 2 \times r \times y$$

Now let us go back to the three squares at the beginning which we wished to compare with the orange square.

We can write the sum of the three squares as $r^2 + g^2 + y^2$ and we have to compare this with o^2.

We form o^2 and place upon it r^2, g^2 and y^2, as in the figure below:

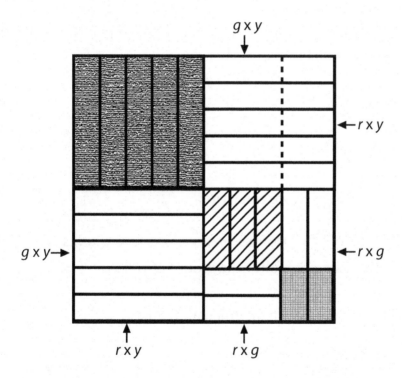

Here we see the three squares and the area of the orange square that is left uncovered. What do we need to cover this?

The dotted lines show us rectangles which we could cover with red, green and yellow rods. Because they can be grouped in pairs equal in area, we can say we need,

2 rectangles each having two green rods or three red rods

2   „   „   „   two yellow rods or five red rods

2   „   „   „   three yellow rods or five green rods

which means that for each of these rectangles we have the crosses or products $r \times g,\ r \times y,\ g \times y$

So we can write:

$$o^2 = r^2 + g^2 + y^2 + 2 \times r \times g + 2 \times r \times y + 2 \times g \times y$$

But, as $o = r + g + y$, we can write:

$$(r + g + y)^2 = r^2 + g^2 + y^2 + 2 \times r \times g + 2 \times r \times y + 2 \times g \times y$$

Repeat this using the following groups of rods:

1   orange, white, red, light green and pink

(Note that $10 = 1 + 2 + 3 + 4$ or $o = w + r + g + p$)

2   blue, red, light green, pink

3   orange, white, red, black

4   blue, white, fight green, yellow.

6 Pyramids

All the games in this section will seem much more difficult when they are written down than they are when played with the rods. So we begin with the rods, seeing what can be done to make changes in the patterns without changing the way in which we proceed. Write down what we have discovered and then we will see how much easier it is to follow what is written in the text.

We have made squares and learned something about them; we shall now study solid bodies and compare them in a similar way.

If we build a pyramid, starting with an orange square at the bottom and decreasing progressively to a white rod at the top and rearrange it so that, at one corner, we have blue rods directly on top of the orange, tan ones on top of the blue and so on, to the top, two sides of the figure we have made will be *vertical* and the other sides will show regular steps. This change in the shape of the figure will not make any change in the volume, though the two shapes are quite different.

We could calculate the volume of each figure by using white rods (each of which has a volume of 1 cubic centimeter or 1 c.c). But we could also calculate the total volume of the figure by first calculating the volume of each layer and then adding the results in the following way:

$$(10^2 + 9^2 + 8^2 + 7^2 + 6^2 + 5^2 + 4^2 + 3^2 + 2^2 + 1^2) \times 1$$

which, read in reverse becomes

$1^2 + 2^2 + \ldots + 9^2 + 10^2$, i.e., the sum of the squares of the first ten numbers.

We can do this step by step:

$1^2 = 1$

$1^2 + 2^2 = 1 + 4 = 5$

$1^2 + 2^2 + 3^2 = 1 + 4 + 9 = 14$

$1^2 + 2^2 + 3^2 + 4^2 = 1 + 4 + 9 + 16 = 30$

$1^2 + 2^2 + 3^2 + 4^2 + 5^2 = 1 + 4 + 9 + 16 + 25 = 55$

and so on, which gives us some interesting relationships.

Let us try out any other game with volumes we can think of; there are plenty of them.

7 Two Interesting Series

Here are some more games that can be played with the rods.

1 Take a white rod. Add three more to it to form a square 2×2. You will see that this can be changed into a square made of two white and one red rod. If you now add five more white rods so as to make a square 3×3, you can replace two of the white rods by a red one and the other three by a light green. Continue in this way adding white rods to make new squares each time and replacing the white rods you have added with two other appropriate rods. The steps will be, 7 white (replaced by light green and pink), 9 white (replaced by pink and yellow) and so on up to 19 white rods (replaced by blue and orange).

At each step we make a square; so we can write down the successive steps we have taken, in numerals:

$$1^2, 2^2, 3^2, 4^2, 5^2, 6^2, 7^2, 8^2, 9^2, 10^2.$$

If we remember that we formed these squares by adding white rods, and the number of white rods needed, we can write:

$$1, 1 + 2, 2 + 3, 3 + 4, 4 + 5 \ldots \text{up to } 9 + 10,$$

and these respectively are equal to,

$$1, 3, 5, 7, 9 \ldots 19.$$

We see that we have written the successive odd numbers, starting with 1.

You already know how to form a series by adding successive odd numbers, stopping at each step. Form one again, and compare it with the series you obtain by squaring the numbers in series of successive numbers from 1 to 10.

1	$= 1^2$
$1 + 3$	$= 2^2$
$1 + 3 + 5$	$= 3^2$
$1 + 3 + 5 + 7$	$= 4^2$
$1 + 3 + 5 + 7 + 9$	$= 5^2$

and so on up to,

$$1 + 3 + 5 + 7 + 9 + 11 + 13 + 15 + 17 + 19 = 10^2.$$

Thus, we can say that the sum of any number of successive odd numbers of which 1 is the first, is equal to the square of the number of numbers to be added. If, for example, we continued the series of odd numbers another 5 steps to obtain 15 terms, the sum of those 15 numbers would be $15^2 = 225$.

2 Take a red rod and border it on two sides with white rods to make a rectangle 2 × 3. You need 4 whites but you could use a light green and a white instead. Thus:

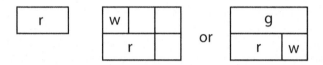

Border this rectangle in the same way on two sides with more whites to make a rectangle 3 × 4, and change these whites for a pink and a red. Continue increasing the rectangle until you find you need an orange and a tan. You need not use whites in these later stages.

The successive rectangles you have made will be expressed in numerals as follows:

2 × 1, 3 × 2, 4 × 3, 5 × 4, 6 × 5, 7 × 6, 8 × 7, 9 × 8, 10 × 9

but, if we look at the rods we have used to border each rectangle we get,

3 + 1, 4 + 2, 5 + 3, 6 + 4, 7 + 5, 8 + 6, 9 + 7, 10 + 8

and these are the successive even numbers from 4 to 18.

Comparing, as before, we find that:

2	$= 1 \times 2$
$2 + 4$	$= 2 \times 3$
$2 + 4 + 6$	$= 3 \times 4$
$2 + 4 + 6 + 8$	$= 4 \times 5$
$2 + 4 + 6 + 8 + 10$	$= 5 \times 6$
$2 + 4 + 6 + 8 + 10 + 12$	$= 6 \times 7$
$2 + 4 + 6 + 8 + 10 + 12 + 14$	$= 7 \times 8$
$2 + 4 + 6 + 8 + 10 + 12 + 14 + 16$	$= 8 \times 9$
$2 + 4 + 6 + 8 + 10 + 12 + 14 + 16 + 18$	$= 9 \times 10$

We can say that the sum of the successive even numbers beginning with 2 is equal to the product of the number of terms we add and the number immediately following. So, if we wished to add all the even numbers from 2 to 40 we should have twenty terms.

$$20 \times 21 = 420$$

Try some examples on your own.

3 The large square which you made in the first of these two games can be separated into two staircases that interlock. One of them, in numerals, is written,

$$1 + 2 + 3 + 4 + 5 + 6 + 7 + 8 + 9 + 10$$

and the other,

$$1 + 2 + 3 + 4 + 5 + 6 + 7 + 8 + 9$$

Similarly, the large rectangle you made in the second game can be separated into two interlocking staircases:

$$2 + 3 + 4 + 5 + 6 + 7 + 8 + 9 + 10$$

and,

$$1 + 2 + 3 + 4 + 5 + 6 + 7 + 8$$

We know that these arrangements give us the sum of the odd numbers and the sum of the even numbers; but would interlocking staircases provide more than the answers to those two questions? Try with the rods and see whether you can do anything else.

This chapter has shown us a few of the many interesting and puzzling games we can play with the rods, and these give us some idea of the numerous possibilities they hold for Johnny who enjoys exploring.

What we must add is that he will also experience the limits of their use, and this is important, too. The most obvious limit results from their being cut in fixed lengths. If we can imagine a set with an immense number of rods, each varying only slightly from the next, we can see how much more could be done. Actually such a set would cover a large slice of the whole of mathematics.

These limits show that paper and pencil are needed and that Johnny must rely upon the use of his own mind. But that is what we wish, because he needs to realize that mathematics is essentially of the mind. So the rods teach him in a two-fold way — by what he finds he can do with them, and by finding, also, the points at which he must go forward by the use of his mental powers alone.

In Textbooks 2, 5, and 7 of *Gattegno Mathematics* the reader will find additional and interesting problems pertaining to the topics studied in this chapter.

6 Helping the Older Child with the Rods

Many readers who can see how valuable the colored rods are for the young child will be asking whether they can help the older Johnny who is meeting difficulties at some later stage in his school career. Can he, also, use the rods to recover his confidence and catch up enough to feel competent in mathematics?

The answer is an emphatic yes.

There is a persistent belief that mathematics is like a ladder and that the missing of a few rungs will lead inevitably to catastrophe. Who has not felt, when returning to school after a long illness, that the other pupils had gone so far ahead that it was no use trying to catch up? The words they were using were so familiar to them and so unfamiliar to us that all was wrapped in mystery.

When this problem arises many parents decide that Johnny must have extra coaching and, in many cases, the additional work and practice give him back at least part of his confidence. Parents understand that the teacher has a course of study to cover and must press on with the class as a whole, whether Johnny can follow or not, and must leave the solution of Johnny's problem to them.

It is not only illness that creates this difficulty. If Johnny's father is transferred from one post to another there will be a change of school. Different methods, a different curriculum, and emotional reactions when faced with new teachers set Johnny a task of adjustment that may lead him to feel inadequate. Even if there is no change of school there are changes of class or Johnny may have a teacher to whom, for a variety of reasons, he does not react well. A temporary loss of interest in the subject can create gaps that leave a continuing discouragement. In most subjects gaps are not as sharply felt as in mathematics and, in this book, we are concerned with helping Johnny to achieve confidence and mastery in that subject. Fortunately, the approach we adopt greatly reduces the importance of this problem of gaps in his knowledge.

If Johnny missed school for some days or if he is unable to follow the usual lessons given at school and parents feel that private coaching will help him, then the approach of this book will be more helpful to him because he is not asked to remember so much but rather to understand thoroughly what he is studying. For memory of something we do not understand, or barely understand, is rarely lasting, whereas we rarely forget what we ourselves do from beginning to end. If we do something properly, it is because we have within ourselves all that is needed to do it, and there is no question of forgetting because it was never a matter of remembering. Since we once lived through it completely, we can relive it again and again.

There are two types of knowledge: one is 'know how' and the other is a record consisting of memory tracks. The first is linked with skill. For example, if I say I know how to write or swim or ride a bicycle, it means that I can do it again even after a long gap. If, on the other hand, I say I know Smith's address or the date of Lincoln's death or of Aunt Gertrude's birthday, I mean only that I have these bits of information stored up in my memory. Moreover, there is another important difference. If I made swimming movements while riding a bicycle the result might be fatal, but if I made a mistake about Aunt Gertrude's birthday it would not be a particularly serious error. It is a piece of information that might well have been different, whereas swimming movements and cycling movements are governed by the nature of the activities themselves and could not be substantially changed.

Mathematical learning in schools is often of the memory-track type, because it is based upon notation. With the rods, properly used, the skill-type of knowledge precedes notation and so gives it its sense.

Children of all ages — from two to eighty-two, as we have observed — immensely enjoy playing with the rods. So the first step is to give Johnny a set of rods and let him play some of the games described in the earlier part of this book. He will be intrigued and will quickly realize that these pieces of colored wood are not a toy for babies to play with. If he is challenged properly he will begin to see that they can help him to think out the problems he has found so difficult.

If, for example, we asked him whether he can make one square with red rods and one with light green rods such that both are equal, a simple manipulation will yield the answer. But if we ask him if he can always find two squares that are equal, each made of one type of rod, the question cannot be solved by manipulation as before. It has become a mathematical question that must be solved by thinking in terms of relationships and formal equivalences. According to Johnny's age and interest he will feel either challenged or bored by this more general question. It will need all the skill of parents and teachers to discern just when such a question can be put.

This is an example of a principle that is most important when using Algebricks. Each question can be put at many levels so that Johnny's stage of development can always be met. This is not so with notational arithmetic, which does not allow of experiment and variations. For example, when Johnny is faced by a question about a man who pays out of his wages 12 % for income tax, 10% for rent, 1.5% for insurance and so on, he either knows how to work it out or he can find nothing in the statement that can assist him. He must search his memory for similar questions and for their stereotyped solution. Johnny is either conditioned to work out such problems or he is helpless.

With the colored rods, Johnny is always asked to experiment first, to make sure that he can see all that is involved in the type of manipulation upon which he is engaged. Only when this process is completed is he asked to formulate his findings in words and in notation. At this stage, he will find that what he knows can be expressed in several ways, but these all correspond with what he has lived through and, therefore, have strong and multiple associations attached to them. When he sees what is written or hears what is said, he recalls everything that makes each step meaningful. Such a question as the one we have just considered contains the clues Johnny needs in order to work out its solution. He does not search his memory but uses his skill in just the same way as he uses it in the other problems he faces in life — resourcefully and confidently.

Now let us be practical and look at some of the points at which Johnny is most likely to need help.

1 Fractions

When a certain mastery has been gained in the games that have occupied us up to this point, Johnny will know that the variety of situations they present is equal to the variety of the questions that face him at school. Let us suppose that Johnny's trouble is caused through missing the first lessons on fractions. His fellows are now adding and subtracting them by a mysterious rule of changing the fractions to the same denominator and then adding or subtracting the new numerators. How can we help Johnny to catch up?

We want him to find his place amongst the able children in his class. So our aim is that Johnny shall, through what he does at home, see that the rule is correct and sums up what he has himself discovered to be true. Any difference between himself and the others will lie in the confidence and ease with which he uses the rule as a result of understanding it.

We show Johnny two rods and ask him to measure one by the other. At first we measure each rod by the white one, taking white as the unit. In this way he names the rods in order as 1, 2, 3 . . . 10, according to the number of whites that make up their lengths. We then use the red rod to measure by and we find that the white is now one half of the red, whereas the light green is three halves, and the pink four halves. Writing down what we have discovered, we get:

$$\frac{1}{2} \quad 1 \quad \frac{3}{2} \quad \frac{4}{2} \quad \frac{5}{2} \quad \frac{6}{2} \quad \frac{7}{2} \quad \frac{8}{2} \quad \frac{9}{2} \quad \frac{10}{2}$$

Johnny soon sees how to name any rod when it is measured by another. When he measures by the light green he will find:

$$\frac{1}{3} \quad \frac{2}{3} \quad \frac{3}{3} \quad \frac{4}{3} \quad \frac{5}{3} \quad \frac{6}{3} \quad \frac{7}{3} \quad \frac{8}{3} \quad \frac{9}{3} \quad \frac{10}{3}$$

Thus, Johnny will know that a yellow measured by a black is five sevenths and that a black measured by a yellow is seven fifths, and he can write $\frac{5}{7}$ or $\frac{7}{5}$ according to which of the two rods he is measuring by. If we now name the bottom number the *denominator* and the top one the *numerator*, he will know that this is the language and the writing that is used at school. He will realize that he is being helped to understand what mystified him there and made him feel so incompetent and unhappy.

Before going further we should observe that in this brief session with Johnny over fractions, we have not appealed to a knowledge he *should* have had. We began from scratch and broke into the heart of his problem, letting him discover what he needed to enable him to move ahead. We did not make him begin as if he had to follow a long course of learning from the rods to reach fractions, but met him at the point of his present need by showing him how the rods could help him at that very point. So, we have proved by this example that mathematics is not like a ladder. We can enter it at various levels. For Johnny what has been added is the understanding of these long words, 'denominator' and 'numerator'; he not only knows what the other children in his class have been told but appreciates, through his own experience, the functions they perform.

Returning to the rods, Johnny can see that not only is the white half the red, but that the red is half the pink, the pink half the tan, and the yellow half the orange. He can write for all these pairs:

$$\frac{2}{4} = \frac{1}{2} \quad \frac{3}{6} = \frac{1}{2} \quad \frac{4}{8} = \frac{1}{2} \quad \frac{5}{10} = \frac{1}{2}$$

Or, to save space he can write:

$$\frac{1}{2} = \frac{2}{4} = \frac{3}{6} = \frac{4}{8} = \frac{5}{10} = \frac{6}{12} \cdots$$

He can repeat the same manipulations with other rods and obtain a number of *equivalent fractions*.

Johnny will see that each time he meets a fraction it is a member of a *family of fractions* all of which are equivalent. So, for a while he can be asked to find the family to which each fraction belongs by writing down some of the members. For example, he can write:

$$\frac{2}{3} = \frac{4}{6} = \frac{6}{9} = \frac{8}{12} = \frac{10}{15} = \cdots$$

and $\quad \frac{3}{5} = \frac{6}{10} = \frac{9}{15} = \frac{12}{20} = \frac{15}{25} = \cdots$

If we give him two pairs of rods, or two fractions, he can, both by manipulation and by notation, find two others which have the same denominator. This is called the *common denominator*. For example, for $\frac{2}{3}$ and $\frac{3}{5}$ he can find from what he has just done that $\frac{10}{15}$ and $\frac{9}{15}$ are two such fractions. If he were to extend the two families by adding more members he would discover $\frac{20}{30}$ and $\frac{18}{30}$, which also have a common denominator, but the fractions with the smallest common denominator in the families of $\frac{2}{3}$ and $\frac{3}{5}$ are $\frac{10}{15}$ and $\frac{9}{15}$. So the *least common denominator* is 15.

Johnny has learned by this that he can always answer questions that require him to replace two fractions by two others having the same denominator and that it makes sense to talk of the least common denominator or L.C.D. of two fractions.

Now we can ask Johnny to compare two fractions and to tell us which is bigger or smaller. The new forms of the fractions which he can find, which have a common denominator, give him the answer at once. He can see that $\frac{10}{15}$ is greater than $\frac{9}{15}$ and he therefore knows that $\frac{2}{3}$ is greater than $\frac{3}{5}$. He would not find it easy to guess the answer by looking at these fractions in notation.

He knows that adding is done by putting rods end to end and finding the name of the new length (using orange rods if necessary), so he agrees that we can find the answer to $\frac{2}{3} + \frac{3}{5}$ like this:

$$\frac{2}{3} + \frac{3}{5} = \frac{10}{15} + \frac{9}{15} = \frac{19}{15}$$

He can even see that:

$$\frac{2}{3} + \frac{3}{5} = \frac{2 \times 5}{3 \times 5} + \frac{3 \times 3}{5 \times 3} = \frac{2 \times 5 + 3 \times 3}{5 \times 3} = \frac{19}{15}$$

This simply tells him what he has been doing all along. Because he knows the steps he himself has taken, he can recall them when he sees them written down and he finds them meaningful.[*]

---

[*] This is the first example met in this book in which we have an addition of two products and as there may be ambiguity in the reading of 2 × 5 + 3 × 3 it is agreed that, if no bracket is inserted to suggest another reading, we multiply a by 5 and 3 by 3 first and then add the results. For more clarity one would have written (2 × 5) + (3 × 3) to distinguish it from 2 × (5 + 3) × 3. The latter always requires the brackets.

After a few such exercises Johnny knows what is to be done when adding or subtracting fractions and what he knows is, in fact, the rule that is taught him at school.

This is only one example of how the older Johnny can be helped. Instead of requiring him to work over exercises and rules we introduce him to what the rods can teach him about the subject at that level and, before long, what bewildered him becomes clear and he grasps what he is being taught at school in such a way that he can rely upon his own skill and understanding and not upon the uncertainties of memory.

2 Those Multiplication Tables!

In an earlier chapter we have shown how Johnny can become a master of his products, but, because it is such an important matter for so many children at all stages, we shall consider it again from a different point of view. What we say now will be useful, whatever age or stage Johnny has reached, if 'learning his tables' is the cause of his dislike of mathematics or of his failure to do well at it, and whether or not he has ever seen the rods previously.

After becoming familiar with the rods by a few minutes of free play we ask Johnny to measure each of them by the white rod. He finds the answers quickly and can soon tell us the number name of each of them. When he knows them we form lengths that include an orange rod, such as an orange and black. Soon he can see that $7 + 10 = 10 + 7$ and why we call that length 17.

Then we give him a length, say 18, and ask him to find all the rods of one color that make a length equal to the length of 18. He finds, after a while, that 2 blue rods, 3 dark green rods, 6 light green rods and 9 red rods are needed and we show him that this can be written $18 = 2 \times 9 = 3 \times 6 = 6 \times 3 = 9 \times 2$. We then ask him to say, with eyes shut, what he must multiply by 6 to get 18, or by 9, 2 or 3.

We agree with him that these four numbers shall be called the factors of 18, and we pair these factors. 2 goes with 9 (and 9 with 2); 3 goes with 6 (and 6 with 3).

To keep them paired, we make crosses — a blue with a red rod across it and a dark green with a light green rod across it. If we reverse the order of the rods in each cross, Johnny can see that its value remains the same. These crosses remind us of the steps we took to find them and, when we are sure that Johnny has accepted the crosses as products in this way, we show him a cross made with a light green rod and a black. He will soon understand that this cross means 3×7 or 7×3 and that, if he makes a length of three black rods and another of seven light green ones they will be equal. Measuring this by orange rods he finds he needs two of them and one white added which, in terms of white rods, is worth 21. $3 \times 7 = 21$ and $7 \times 3 = 21$.

We give Johnny some more crosses and each time he can find the answer and express it in notation. As we add new crosses, we repeat ones he has seen before. So, after the first session he will, perhaps, know that $2 \times 9 = 3 \times 6 = 18$, that $3 \times 7 = 21$, and that $4 \times 10 = 8 \times 5 = 40$. He will probably know a few more as well. At the next session we shall begin with these and add a few more.

This game can be continued with crosses but it is valuable to have the cardboard materials with their symbols in which only the colors appear. Johnny readily accepts the convention that yellow means 5 and black 7. He knows that 5 black rods and 7 yellow rods make equal lengths and that he can read the yellow/black symbol $5 \times 7 = 35$ or as $7 \times 5 = 35$.

If Johnny has the wall chart in which all the products are arranged, he can recognize the few he knows and will see others that are still unfamiliar. But the rest, except for three isolated examples (black/black, blue/blue and black/blue), are linked by very simple relationships with one another. One may be double another, or half, or double the double, or half of half. These relationships help Johnny to visualize the answers by seeing them in a pattern which is easy to follow. He need not learn each product by itself for he can come to know them in their related groups. He finds that 7×10 is 70, which is also twice 35, and that 64 is twice 32, which is twice 16, which is twice 8 and so on.

When Johnny can recognize all the products on the wall chart, he will have the means of finding and knowing many more products than are usually learned at school and, instead of asking him to memorize tables, we can let him produce the tables for us. All he need do is to find all the products in which a red rod is represented and write them down in order to make the table: $2 \times 2 = 4$, $3 \times 2 = 6$, $4 \times 2 = 8$ and so on up to $10 \times 2 = 20$. Taking, next, all the products containing light green he will produce the table: $2 \times 3 = 6$, $3 \times 3 = 9$, $4 \times 3 = 12$ and so on up to $10 \times 3 = 30$. By taking the other colors in order he forms all the tables from $2 \times 2 = 4$ to $10 \times 10 = 100$.

By this method, the multiplication tables come at the end, *after* the products and their factors are known. He does not need to use the tables or learn them but, if his teacher requires him to know them, Johnny can show that he knows them as well as anyone else in his class. Indeed, he may know many more products than his fellows and he has the means for adding more whenever he wishes. He certainly need not stop at $12 \times 12 = 144$, as is so commonly done in schools.

3 Subtraction

Earlier in this book we spoke of Johnny's difficulties when required to learn subtraction by the usual methods, and we have already taken the first step towards ensuring that these difficulties will not trouble him. By placing rods or lengths of rods side by side he has realized that subtraction means the finding of a *difference*. If he has placed an orange and white rod end to end with a blue rod side by side he has seen that the difference is the length of a red rod. In numerals he has written this as $11 - 9 = 2$.

If he lengthens the two lines by adding the same number of orange rods to each on the left, or by adding any rods on the right in equal lengths, he will find that the difference remains the same. Suppose he adds an orange rod to each line on the left to obtain 21 − 19 = 2, and then a white one to each on the right; he obtains 22 − 20 = 2. This can be shown equally well as (two orange rods and a red) side by side with two orange rods. But however it is shown, the difference remains the length of one red rod.

If Johnny is now asked to write what he has been doing in vertical notation he can do so easily and can find an even simpler expression of what he has learned about *equivalent differences*, which appears as the last example below:

$$\begin{array}{cccc} 11 & 21 & 22 & 2 \\ -9 & -19 & -20 & -0 \\ \hline 2 & 2 & 2 & 2 \end{array}$$

When written in this way the first two forms seem to be more difficult than the last two, especially the second; but the equivalence is clear.

By the usual methods, Johnny might be taught to overcome the problem created by the new notation by 'borrowing' and 'paying back'; but how much simpler and clearer it is to form an equivalent difference by adding 1 to the two numbers! He can do this perfectly easily in his head and get the right answer at once.

Here is another example which Johnny can do equally well:

$$
\begin{array}{r@{\qquad}r@{\qquad}r}
273 & 275 & 75 \\
-198 & -200 & -0 \\
\hline
75 & 75 & 75
\end{array}
$$

The first looks difficult. The second is easy, and the third is ridiculously easy. So why does Johnny need to learn any notational tricks to do such subtractions?

Now, if we combine the two examples we get:

$$
\begin{array}{r@{\quad}r@{\ }r}
21273 & 22275 & 2275 \\
-19198 & -20200 & -200 \\
\hline
2075 & 2075 & 2075
\end{array}
$$

These are equivalent differences again and, by breaking down the subtraction into two parts and finding easy equivalent differences, Johnny can readily solve the apparently difficult subtraction–and he enjoys doing it because it is an interesting challenge, and he can see just what is happening. He is using his intelligence instead of blindly following a complicated rule.

Even if Johnny knew no more than this, he would be able to tackle the subtractions that come his way. He would break them up and add or subtract rapidly in his head as required to find the answer. He would learn to look on such operations as a whole, using his understanding of equivalent differences to meet every case. But let us suppose the teacher gives him a very long subtraction with all the difficulties he can devise to defeat Johnny to show that he *must* know one of the methods usually taught. Will he have the answer? Here is a 'very hard' subtraction.

940031200572
– 776439804785

In this example almost all the figures below cannot be subtracted from the figures above. If he were to try to work it out by 'borrowing' and 'paying back' he would discover that at certain points there would be 'neighbors' with nothing to 'lend.' This has been called the famous 'o' difficulty! But Johnny can see that if he adds equal numbers to both these big numbers he could form the easy subtraction:

963591395787
– 800000000000

Of course, he cannot form this equivalent difference in his head, but he need not work it out separately on paper, for, because of what he has discovered, he can not only easily find the answer by working from right to left but he can do it equally confidently from left to right. Here is the difference again in its difficult form so that Johnny can follow what is explained below:

940031200572
– 776439804785
  163591395787

His task is to increase the two big numbers mentally so that the bottom one becomes an 8 with a string of zeros, moving the top one up by an equivalent amount. He begins with the 5 at the right. He must increase it by 5 to reach zero, and so he must add 5 to the number above. He thus gives himself the simple subtraction $7 - 0 = 7$ and writes down 7 as the first figure of the answer.

But by increasing this 5 by 5 he has produced 10, so the 8 next door has become 9. (If Johnny watches a speedometer move up as the miles go by he will understand this very easily.) To bring 9 to o, he must add 1, and the 7 above becomes 8, $8 - 0 = 8$, so the next figure in the answer is 8.

As he works step by step from right to left, Johnny notices that whenever he has to move a figure up to zero he is really bringing it up to 10, so that the figure on the left is always increased by 1. He notices that the first figure on the right is not increased in that way but that all the rest are. When he comes to the figure on the extreme left he knows it is increased by 1 but sees that he can subtract it from the number above at once. So Johnny can astonish his friends by doing the subtraction from left to right as easily as from right to left. Indeed he can fill in the figures of the answer at random, knowing that each one is correct. He can also check any individual figure if he thinks he has made a slip.

If Johnny begins with the rods and is quite clear about equivalent differences, he will move from stage to stage without encountering any problem. Each stage will be simple and obvious and each will provide him with a new set of games he can play with figures he himself chooses. Surprisingly quickly (if he is allowed to proceed at his own pace) he will tackle long and complicated subtractions with real enjoyment because he has a complete understanding of what he is doing.

4 Advanced Work

If Johnny is beyond the elementary stage he may not be very happy if he is asked to play games that younger children enjoy playing with the rods; yet it may be lack of experience with products, factors, subtraction and fractions that accounts for his failure and his dislike of mathematics.

What can we do about this older Johnny who wishes to be treated as a fourth or fifth former?

If he is given Textbook 5 or any of those that follow, he will realize that the rods are not for babies, because these books will stretch his powers to the utmost and there is no reason why he should not come to know the rods through the challenges they present. He will find that he needs to know how to form towers and why these represent factors and multiplications, but he can do this while practicing *powers*, finding out the laws of indices, or even while discovering how to work in bases other than ten, which he will find most fascinating.

He will soon be convinced that it is worth playing the games of identification and practicing multiplication, division, subtractions by the method of equivalent differences, and many other things found in this book. He will find that he can make them all as difficult as he wishes, because the remarkable feature of this material is that each situation created with the rods can be explored at many levels and the older Johnny may be studying the same pattern as the younger child but for a purpose that the younger one will be unable to tackle for a number of years.

To explain all that can be discovered and mastered by the older boy or girl cannot be undertaken in a book of this size, but the textbooks are written primarily for the student and can be used without a teacher by any child or young person whose enthusiasm for mathematics has been kindled by the rods.

In the last chapter we shall explain why the rods provide the solution to all of Johnny's worries and, therefore, to his parents' anxiety.

In Textbook 2 of *Gattegno Mathematics* there is special work dealing with procedures and algorithms for addition, subtraction, multiplication and division. In Textbook 4 one finds a complete treatment of fractions.

7 Why All This Works So Well

Having completed this pleasant journey in the field of mathematics, Johnny's parents may wish to ask why this new approach is so effective and why, since it seems so simple, we had to wait so long to find a solution to Johnny's problems in learning arithmetic.

Mathematicians are rather proud of their logical thinking and, for them, numbers are formed of the unit added to itself repeatedly. This simple assumption is apparent from the character of all the teaching aids that were devised before colored rods were invented, for all of them were essentially devices for counting. It now seems obvious that no mathematician could have thought of the rods because Cuisenaire's invention rested upon his rejection of the dominance of the unit.

But this does not explain the value of his discovery. In fact, in contrast to what can be said about the many other aids, the unique success of the rods is the result of numerous factors, and we can here mention only a few of them:

1   Johnny, being the source of his own knowledge, no longer relies upon someone else's knowledge or mental processes and his mind is far freer.

2   Because his understanding of number behavior is based upon his own activity and the operation of his own senses, he can *experience* the validity of every statement he makes.

3   By finding mathematical relationships in the course of this activity with the rods, and then expressing what he has found in terms that make sense to him, the traditional notation gains an immediate meaning for him, and is not something foreign to his experience imposed from outside.

4   As the same activity is valid both in the study of whole numbers and of fractions, Johnny no longer supposes that he must recast all his knowledge when he passes from one to the other. What he already knows is found to apply in the new field, which is seen to be only an extension of the field that is already familiar.

5   All mathematical processes are presented as facets of the games he has enjoyed playing with the rods, so that there is a continuous and coherent enlightenment as Johnny's mathematic insight develops.

6   Mathematics ceases to be a ladder to be climbed, rung by rung, for Johnny is able to make his entry into the subject by way of a number of games, each of which gives him mathematical experience. Moreover, he can always start from scratch when approaching new topics, and can move from one field to another, using the experience he has gained to illuminate the new field. For example, division can be derived direct from addition and does not require the knowledge of multiplication tables as before.

7   Within the patterns that Johnny so easily makes he reads many interrelated mathematical processes, all of which are seen as aspects of a single mathematical truth, and he realizes that mathematics is a thing of the mind. He quickly reaches a high level of competence and he develops initiative. His mistakes are usually slips which he himself can correct and, accordingly, his confidence is not undermined by the errors he makes.

8   Relying upon the deeper levels of memory that are made up of numerous relationships, instead of resting upon the shallow memory tracks established by verbal repetition and the drill of tedious exercises, Johnny is never at a loss when he encounters a situation which, in some aspect, is related to something he has already mastered. He moves from the known to the unknown by the aid of the rods and what they have revealed to him, so that, instead of being fearful of the unfamiliar, he is stimulated by it. The experience of change gives him keen pleasure and his initiative is constantly strengthened.

No doubt every reader will add to these reasons others of his own, and may even feel that the most important ones have been omitted from this list. This is in the nature of things because, for centuries, mathematicians have noticed new relationships in their fields of study, and the set of rods represents a *model* of a large part of mathematics. It is not surprising, therefore, that they perpetually reveal new aspects of their value and stir up new ideas. Thus, anyone who plays with them is likely to find new uses and perceive new values and this, perhaps, is the reason that embraces all the others. So let this be added as the final one in our list:

9   The set of colored rods is a true model of elementary algebra, allowing Johnny to discover in it all that he finds in his school books and much that is omitted from them because it is too difficult to explain with the ordinary tools possessed by the ordinary teacher.

CPSIA information can be obtained
at www.ICGtesting.com
Printed in the USA
BVOW09s0522141216
470264BV00006B/15/P